Times of Refreshing

G000075771

Autumn
Devotional

Ruth Gregg

O&U
Onwards & Upwards

Onwards and Upwards Publishers

3 Radfords Turf, Cranbrook, Exeter,
EX5 7DX, United Kingdom.
www.onwardsandupwards.org

First edition, published in the United Kingdom by Onwards and Upwards Publishers (2020).

ISBN:	978-1-78815-704-9
Typeface:	Sabon LT
Graphic design:	LM Graphic Design

Every effort has been made by the author to obtain the necessary permissions to reproduce copyrighted material. If, however, there have been any omissions or errors, please contact the publisher to have these corrected in future reprints and editions.

The views and opinions expressed in this book are the author's own, and do not necessarily represent the views and opinions of Onwards and Upwards Publishers or its staff.

Endorsements

Times of Refreshing does what it says on the tin – it is full to overflowing with spiritual refreshment. At a time when spiritual attentiveness and soul care can be such easily neglected spiritual disciplines, due to the busy demands made on our lives by so many other things, this spiritually anointed and biblically literate gem of Ruth's is pure gold. It is a collection of inspiring and deeply personal devotionals which come out of a heart which has been captivated by the Father's amazing love and longs for deep personal and national revival – you will certainly meet the Saviour in its pages.

Rev. Daniel Kane
West Presbyterian Church, Ballymena

There are often times in the normal day-to-day hectic schedule of ministry life that you run out of steam and need to have a pit-stop. Sadly, I am on first name terms with a lot of the deli-counter staff and hot food staff all over Ballymena! This also can be said of our walk with God; we can run out of steam and need a pit-stop. In *Times of Refreshing*, Ruth has provided the perfect spiritual pick-me-up – a devotional that can allow us to pause, rest for a while, have a spiritual snack and recharge our batteries. Better than any meal deal, *Times of Refreshing* will help us run our race and fight our battles. In fact, why don't you get your copy and keep it where you work and make it part of your daily pit-stop routine? Ruth, thank you for this gift. My prayer, like yours, is that many will find essential daily spiritual refreshing as they use *Times of Refreshing*.

Rev. Mark McConnell
Rector, Ballymena Parish Church

There is nothing quite as good for any of us as to spend the first part of the day meditating on the Word of God. As I have read through this beautiful devotional that Ruth has written, I know that many lives will be refreshed and encouraged. Ruth has brought fresh revelation on the Scriptures and nuggets of truth that you can ponder on throughout the day. I highly recommend this book as a tool for anyone who hungers for more of God.

Pastor Roy Stewart
Pastor, Celebration House, Ballymena

About the Author

 Ruth has been involved in ministry for the past thirty years. She holds a B.D. from Queens University, a Doctorate in Biblical Studies from CLU, has released various print publications, and currently resides in County Antrim, Northern Ireland. She is director of Impact Unlimited Bible College and CTTW, a 24/7 global prayer initiative.

Her passion is to inspire others through writing in a way that is insightful, meaningful and relevant. In the *Times of Refreshing* devotionals, she taps into her experiences as a pastor, teacher, wife and mother of two, to relate poignant stories from real-life experiences.

To contact the author, please write to:

Ruth Gregg
c/o Onwards and Upwards Publishers Ltd.
3 Radfords Turf
Exeter
EX5 7DX

More information about the author can be found at:

www.onwardsandupwards.org/ruth-gregg

Foreword by Tommy Stewart

Times of Refreshing is a devotional full of life-changing words of inspiration and encouragement written by Dr Ruth Gregg, drawn from a lifetime of study of God's Word. The devotional has been written to encourage the reader to trust God in every circumstance of life and to give the reader courage each day to step out in faith, believing that God is with them and has good plans for their lives.

I have known Dr Ruth Gregg from our college days when Ruth was studying Theology and I was studying Economics. My earliest impressions were of someone deeply committed to the study of God's Word and to being able to communicate it in such a way that the Word of God came alive in the life of the hearer. Through Ruth's ministry, both as a pastor and a teacher, she has shown herself to be "a worker who does not need to be ashamed and who correctly handles the Word of truth" (2 Tim. 2:15). Her dedication to creating teaching materials for pastors in the 10/40 window and her passion for revival mean that Ruth's writings are filled with great truths, anointed by the Holy Spirit.

If, like me, you have struggled to read and meditate daily on what the Bible has to say, then *Times of Refreshing* will provide you with the opportunity to develop a daily rhythm of reading and meditating on the truth of God's Word.

It is said that it takes twenty-one days to develop a habit. I can think of few better habits that you could develop than creating space each day, with the help of *Times of Refreshing*, to be refreshed by God's Word.

I wonder, can you answer yes to any of the following questions?

- Do you want to have a deeper sense of God's peace?
- Do you want to grow closer to God?
- Do you want to be more like Jesus?
- Do you want to know more of God's Word?
- Do you want to grow in confidence in who you are in Christ?

Then, be assured, *Times of Refreshing* is for you!

Tommy Stewart
Founder/Director, Christians Who Lead

September

September

1

Autumnal Abscission

And throwing off his cloak, he sprang up and came to Jesus.

Mark 10:50 (ESV)

As we enter the autumnal season of "mists and mellow fruitfulness"[1], one of the highlights is surely watching the leaves, a riot of gold and red, pirouetting down from their boughs above to quilt the landscape beneath. But have you ever wondered why deciduous trees lose their leaves? I'm told that shedding leaves helps trees to conserve water and energy. Without dropping leaves, a tree would be stuck with thousands of unproductive appendages. Many leaves are insect-eaten, diseased or otherwise damaged. Dropping them gives the plant a fresh start. How then does it happen? As unfavourable weather approaches, hormones in the trees trigger the process of abscission whereby the leaves are actively cut off from the tree by specialised cells. The noun 'abscission' is of Latin origin and was first used in fifteenth century English as a word to describe the act or process of cutting off. It shares the same Latin root as that in scissors, *scindere*, which means 'to cut'. The process of abscission, which applies to petals and fruit as well as leaves, is also how stags cast off their antlers after the rut and snakes shed their skins.

At this time of year as we visibly observe the trees shedding their leaves, it's an excellent opportunity to examine ourselves and cast off any unproductive appendages in our lives. Hebrews 12:1 tells us to "throw off everything that hinders and the sin that so easily entangles"[2] or as The Voice translation phrases it, "…let us drop every extra weight, every sin that clings to us and slackens our pace."[3] What is depleting your energy? What is distracting your attention from Jesus? What is weighing down

---

[1] John Keats; *To Autumn*
[2] NIVUK
[3] TVT

your heart? What negative thought patterns are adversely affecting your walk with God? The Bible says to "throw [it] off"[4] or "throw [it] aside"[5] it. The Greek word used here is *apotithimi*, a compound of the words *apo* and *tithimi*. *Apo* means 'away' and *tithimi* means 'to lay something down'. The idea is to deliberately lay down what hinders and permanently push it far away out of reach.

We read that Bartimaeus threw off his cloak, but why did Mark even acknowledge the coat when he wrote this Gospel? Why was that significant? The garment or cloak was a visual cue for a blind person or beggar. It lay it on the ground to collect alms. Bartimaeus immediately throws it all away and he responds to Jesus' question, "What do you want me to do for you?"[6] with the answer, "My teacher, let me see again."[7] It's the same question that the disciples got in verse 36, but a very different answer. Jesus says, "Go; your faith has made you well."[8] Immediately Bartimaeus regains his sight and follows him on the way. Discarding his cloak was a deliberate act of faith.

By faith may we throw off whatever 'weights' are holding us back and allow the Holy Spirit to highlight any areas which need the process of 'abscission' this autumn.

---

4 ESV
5 NASB
6 ESV
7 NRSV
8 NASB

2

The Mercy Seat

And there I will meet with thee, and I will commune with thee from above the Mercy Seat.

Exodus 25:22 (KJV)

From time to time I watch a programme on television which addresses behavioural problems in children and helps by offering practical advice to beleaguered parents. It seeks to discipline unruly children using what is referred to as the 'naughty seat'. This form of discipline is especially popular in Western cultures. If your child misbehaves, you give him a warning. If he ignores it, you take him to the naughty seat and explain why he's there. After a time period you go back to the seat and expect an apology.

Our verse today mentions another seat called "the Mercy Seat". It is mentioned more than twenty times in the Bible, but its first mention is in Exodus 25:17-22.

You shall make a mercy seat of pure gold; two and a half cubits shall be its length and a cubit and a half its width. And you shall make two cherubim of gold; of hammered work you shall make them at the two ends of the mercy seat.

Exodus 25:17-18 (NKJV)

The Hebrew word for "mercy seat" is *kaphoreth,* from the verb *kphr* meaning 'cover over, pacify, make propitiation', and is related to the word for 'atonement', which is *kippur.* The Greek word for "mercy seat"[9] mentioned in Hebrews 9:5 is *hilasterion,* which means 'that which makes expiation' or 'propitiation'. It comes from the Greek word *hilasmos,* meaning 'the means by which sins are forgiven', and is itself defined as 'the means or place where sins are forgiven'. It carries the idea of the removal of sin. It was a "seat" of mercy in that it was the place

---

9   NASB

where mercy, propitiation[10] and expiation[11] took place. The New Testament uses this word twice: the first in reference to the items of the tabernacle,[12] and the second in reference to Jesus and translated as "atonement".

> *...for all have sinned and fall short of the glory of God, and all are justified freely by his grace through the redemption that came by Christ Jesus. God presented Christ as a sacrifice of atonement, through the shedding of his blood.*
>
> Romans 3:23-25 (NIV)

God promised that He would "meet with" His people and "speak to"[13] them from the mercy seat, between the cherubim.

> *There I will meet with you and, from above the mercy seat, from between the two cherubim that are upon the ark of the Testimony, I will speak intimately with you...*
>
> Exodus 25:22 (AMPC)

While we all deserve to be on the 'naughty seat' because of our sins, the mercy seat speaks to us of mercy and atonement and points us to Jesus. The price of sin has been paid in full by the blood of Jesus and we can come into God's Presence and commune with Him. Hebrews 10:19,22 assures us:

> *Therefore, brethren, since we have confidence to enter the holy place by the blood of Jesus, ... let us draw near with a sincere heart in full assurance of faith.*
>
> Hebrews 10:19,22 (NASB)

Thank God for the mercy seat.

---

[10] Propitiation meaning: Latin *propitius* (favourable). God moves from being at enmity with us to being for us.

[11] Expiation meaning: Latin *expiare*, *ex-* ('out') + *piare* ('to atone'). Something has been taken away, i.e. our sin; our debt is paid through the work of Jesus on the Cross.

[12] See Hebrews 9:1-5

[13] NASB

3

The Best Medicine – Laughter

A merry heart doeth good like a medicine: but a broken spirit drieth the bones.

Proverbs 17:22 (KJV)

Everyone's laugh is unique; they are all slightly different, from giggles to guffaws and from chuckles to cackles. Charlie Chaplin once said, "A day without laughter is a day wasted." On average, children laugh four hundred times a day, while adults laugh about fifteen times. Why the gap? Did we lose something? In the thirteenth century, surgeons used humour to distract patients during surgery. Today, laughter or 'humour therapy' is employed by a variety of hospitals to help patients handle pain.

It is often said that "laughter is the best medicine", and it's true!

A cheerful disposition is good for your health; gloom and doom leave you bone-tired.

Proverbs 17:22 (MSG)

It turns out there's some scientific veracity behind the old adage "laughter is the best medicine". In fact, the science of laughing and its effects on the body is referred to as gelotology. A good, hearty laugh decreases stress hormones, leaving your muscles relaxed for up to forty-five minutes after. Laughter increases immune cells and infection-fighting antibodies, thus improving your resistance to disease. It increases our pain threshold. It triggers the release of endorphins, the body's natural feel-good chemicals. Endorphins promote an overall sense of well-being and can even temporarily relieve pain. Watching just fifteen minutes of comedy makes us 10% more resistant to pain. Laughter triggers the right side of the brain, which helps release creativity and helps us to make better decisions. Laughter activates the body's natural tranquillisers that not only help us to calm down, but even to sleep better. Laughing is a pretty good workout! When you laugh, you are strengthening muscles in your face, stomach and diaphragm. For every fifteen minutes of solid full-body laughing you do, you can burn up to forty calories! (You would have to laugh solidly for up to three hours to burn off a packet of ready salted crisps.)

According to Allen Klein from the Association for Applied and Therapeutic Humour:

> *Your attitude is like a box of crayons that colour the world. Constantly use grey colours, and your picture will always be dark and depressing. Use humour to add bright colours, and your picture begins to lighten up.*

Laughter really is contagious. Ever wonder why television shows often play a 'laugh track' after a funny moment? Even when we do not see where the source of the laughter is, simply hearing laughter can be contagious. It should be noted, laughter is 100% free! It has no side effects. You can take it as often as you like. So, make sure you're taking your medicine!

4

United or Untied?

Behold, how good and how pleasant it is for brethren to dwell together in unity!

Psalm 133:1 (KJV)

The same letters are used to form both words, but which do you prefer – 'united' or 'untied'? United speaks of unity, harmony, agreement. Untied speaks of disunity, fragmentation, division and disagreement. The word 'united' is the popular choice; for example, United States, United Airlines, United Nations and footballs clubs adopt the name United. In Psalm 133, part of the Songs of Ascents which pilgrims sang on their way to the Passover, Pentecost and Feast of Tabernacles in Jerusalem, David wrote about the subject of unity.

The psalm ends with a promise:

...for there the LORD commanded the blessing, even life for evermore.

Psalm 133:3 (KJV)

David affirms the beauty of unity. He declares it to be both good and pleasant. It is good in that it is pleasing to God, and it is pleasant in that it brings delight and happiness to those who experience it. Not all Bible translations have it, but in the Hebrew there is an actual "Behold!" at the beginning of the verse. The goodness of living together in unity is so good that the psalmist says, "Behold! Look! Marvel at what I am about to describe to you!" He compares unity to oil in verse 2:

It is like precious oil poured on the head...

Psalm 133:2 (NIV)

The oil spoken of is the anointing oil of which the Bible gives specific ingredients and quantities to be used: myrrh, cinnamon, calamus, cassia mixed with the oil of the olive. All these elements mixed together became one oil used in the anointing of people in ministry and the vessels of the sanctuary. The ingredients purposefully blended together and flowed as one.

Paul wrote:

> *I appeal to you, brothers and sisters, in the name of our Lord Jesus Christ, that all of you agree with one another in what you say and that there be no divisions among you, but that you be perfectly united in mind and thought.*
>
> *1 Corinthians 1:10 (NIV)*

Unity is absolutely essential because the church is the body of Christ, not a disjointed group of individuals. The secret to unity begins with how we view ourselves within the body and how we view others. Disunity within a church can usually be traced back to the simple truth that too often people act selfishly looking to their own needs, their own desires and their own greeds. James put it:

> *For wherever there is jealousy and selfish ambition, there you will find disorder and evil of every kind.*
>
> *James 3:16*

Division comes when we think 'my empire', 'me, I and myself'. However, we should be Kingdom-minded and think of God's Kingdom. God has called us to build His Kingdom, not our individual empires. Paul stated:

> *Always be humble and gentle. Be patient with each other, making allowance for each other's faults because of your love. Make every effort to keep yourselves united in the Spirit, binding yourselves together with peace. For there is one body and one Spirit, just as you have been called to one glorious hope for the future.*
>
> *Ephesians 4:2-4*

God does not want us to be untied; He wants us to be united and experience the blessing of unity.

5

Gifted

Since we have gifts that differ according to the grace given to us, each of us is to use them accordingly ... he who gives, with liberality; he who leads, with diligence; he who shows mercy, with cheerfulness.

Romans 12:6,8 (NASB)

*P*aul says that we all have different gifts. Your gift is a God-given capacity to fulfil what He has asked you to accomplish. Your spiritual gifts are ultimately designed to bring glory to God and edify others. Paul writes:

...he who gives, with generosity; he who leads, with diligence; he who shows mercy [in caring for others], with cheerfulness.

Romans 12:8 (AMP)

We don't just give or lead or show mercy. We do it with liberality/ generosity, with diligence and with cheerfulness. How important are these descriptors!

It is not simply giving – it is giving with liberality. It is giving which is sincere – heartfelt giving that is untainted by affectation or ulterior motive. The gift of giving is not limited to financial giving. As Peter said:

Silver or gold I do not have, but what I have I give you...

Acts 3:6 (BSB)

You can give of your talents, time, as well as treasure. When you give, do it as Jesus commanded:

Freely you have received, freely give.

Matthew 10:8 (NASB)

The Christian who gives with liberality gives *of* himself, not *for* himself. He does not give for thanks or recognition, but for the sake of the one who receives his help and for the glory of the Lord.

The one who is placed in a position of authority or leadership should carry out his or her duties with "diligence". This word refers to eagerness, earnestness, willingness or zeal. There is no room for laziness or lethargy.

Again, when we show mercy, we should exhibit cheerfulness. Paul's addendum of cheerfulness is no small matter. Wuest in his translation says:

> *...the one who shows mercy, with a joyous abandon.*
>
> *Romans 12:8*

The perfect example of mercy without cheerfulness is that of Job's 'comforters' who poured even more gloom on Job's circumstances. People who are suffering can tell whether you're there helping them as a duty or because you genuinely delight to care for them. They don't need to hear about how much you're sacrificing to help them. They need a cheerful countenance.

Imagine the difference if we did everything today with cheer and diligence and liberality.

6

Made Accepted

...to the praise of the glory of His grace, by which He made us accepted in the Beloved...

Ephesians 1:6 (NKJV)

Too many people are plagued with insecurity and a sense of inadequacy. Many spend their entire lives trying to earn acceptance and approval from parents, peers, partners in life and people they respect. They wrestle for acceptance rather than rest in the finished work of Christ. Many have been deceived into thinking they must somehow earn acceptance in the eyes of God. The Bible, however, tells us that there is nothing in us, nor in what we do, that can in any way merit God's love and favour. Rather, Paul said:

...He hath made us accepted in the beloved.

Ephesians 1:6 (KJV)

Trying to understand *why* God accepts us may baffle our minds, but the *how* is clear. "He made us accepted in the Beloved." It's only in Christ – in the Beloved – that we are who we are! It's all about Jesus! C. H. Spurgeon commented on the words "accepted in the Beloved" saying:

Are there grander words in any language than these four?

Hedley Vicars said:

What a healing balm is there here, for a weary, heavy-laden sinner!

Close your eyes for a moment and tell yourself over and over, "I am accepted in the Beloved." This speaks of our justification, of Christ's righteousness credited to our account by grace through faith.

The verb "accepted" (*charitoo* in Greek) is derived from the word for 'grace' (*charis*) and could be read, "God has begraced us with His grace in the Beloved." The word literally means 'pursue with grace, compass with favour and honour with blessings'! Isn't that lovely? God has pursued you with grace, encompassed you with favour and honoured you with blessings! The verb occurs in only one other New Testament passage, Luke 1:28, where the angel greets the Mary with the words:

> *Hail, thou that art <u>highly favoured</u> among women.*
>
> *Luke 1:28 (KJV, emphasis added)*

We are a highly favoured people today, superabundantly loved and wholly approved, pursued with grace, encompassed with favour and honoured with blessings!

Paul writes to the Romans and further states:

> *Therefore, accept each other just as Christ has accepted you so that God will be given glory.*
>
> *Romans 15:7 (NLT)*

If we don't know we are accepted in the Beloved, then we are going to have trouble accepting others. Hurt people hurt people. The key phrase for understanding and practising this command is the phrase, "just as Christ has accepted you". There is no reason to compete with others when you already know you are complete in Christ. The same grace that has been shown to me, I must show to others by being gracious. The same extravagant love that has been poured into my life should pour through my life to others. It is the same principle mentioned by John:

> *We love because He first loved us.*
>
> *1 John 4:19 (BSB)*

The only reason you can love God or anybody else is because God first loved you. As Paul taught:

> *Be ye kind one to another, tenderhearted, forgiving one another, even as God for Christ's sake hath forgiven you.*
>
> *Ephesians 4:32 (KJV)*

May we accept others just as Christ has accepted us. In this way God will be given glory.

7

Carpe Diem

But encourage one another day after day, as long as it is still
called "Today"...

Hebrews 3:13 (NASB)

*Y*ou would probably be surprised by how much Latin you actually know. Hundreds of words – like memo, alibi, agenda, census, veto, alias, via, alumni, vice versa and per annum – are all used in everyday English, as are abbreviations like i.e. (*id est,* 'that is') and etc. (*et cetera,* 'and the rest'). You may well be familiar with the Latin phrases, *Agnus Dei* – 'Lamb of God'; *bona fide* – 'in good faith, sincerely'; *Dei Gratia* – 'by the grace of God'. In all likelihood you will have heard of *persona non grata* ('unwelcome person'); *curriculum vitae* ('a lengthened resume') and *verbatim* ('in the exact same words'). Possibly your old school motto was in Latin too. Mine was *Per laborem,* meaning 'Through, or by means of, work'.

Let's consider another Latin term, *Carpe diem.* Have you heard of that before now? It means 'Seize the day'. *Carpe diem* is from a poem written in Latin by Horace *(Odes I.xi).* It literally means 'pluck the day' as in plucking fruit which is ripe. The point of the poem was that a person does not know what the future holds so one should make the most of what a person has at the moment. But what does seizing the day mean in the Bible? Let's check out a few examples.

> *This is the day the LORD has made.*
> *We will rejoice and be glad in it.*

Psalm 118:24 (NLT)

So often we focus on the disappointments of yesterday or the uncertainties of tomorrow and miss God's matchless gift to us: *Today.* Each day is a rich and precious gift from God, with new grace and new opportunities. He tells us, today is a day for salvation.

Today, if you hear his voice, do not harden your hearts.

Hebrews 4:7 (NIV)

Behold, now is the acceptable time; behold, now is the day of salvation.

2 Corinthians 6:2 (ERV)

Jesus said to Zacchaeus:

"Today salvation has come to this house..."

Luke 19:9 (NIV)

Today is the day of grace, the day in which salvation through faith in the Lord Jesus Christ is still readily available. God says:

See, I set before you today life and prosperity, death and destruction. ... Now choose life, so that you and your children may live.

Deuteronomy 30:15,19 (NIV)

The decisions and choices we make today are crucial for eternity! Today is ripe with new opportunities to come alongside someone and speak words of encouragement. It is easy to live in the past. It is easy to dream away the future. It's a real challenge to face the present and take advantage of the blessing of each day. *Carpe diem* – seize the day! Live life to the fullest, getting the most out of each individual day to the glory of God.

8

Ampersand Day

Let us think of ways to motivate one another to acts of love and good works. And let us not neglect our meeting together, as some people do, but encourage one another, especially now that the day of his return is drawing near.

Hebrews 10:24-25

September 8 is National Ampersand Day in the US. The ampersand – &, which stands for 'and' – is a great symbol. The unique '&' character, situated above the '7' on the keyboard, is a favourite of grammar lovers, typographers and graphic designers alike. You will notice it in famous brands and logos: Johnson & Johnson, Barnes & Noble, Dolce & Gabbana, clothing brand H&M etc. From jotting a shorthand 'and' to branding corporate names, this curly little character is ubiquitously useful.

Where did this quirky, aesthetically pleasing character come from? Its shape predates the name ampersand by more than 1,500 years. In the first century, Roman scribes wrote in cursive, so when they wrote the Latin word *et* which means 'and', they linked the 'e' and 't'. Scribes wrote so quickly that the letters blended together, thus giving us '&'. Over time the combined letters came to signify the word 'and' in English as well. The first ampersand sign dates back to 79 AD in the ancient town of Pompeii. The '&' has been found etched into some of the ruins that survived the eruption of Mount Vesuvius. The symbol '&' was actually part of the English alphabet in the early 1800s. At that time, school children reciting their ABCs concluded the alphabet with the & as the twenty-seventh part of the alphabet. They would sing, "...X, Y, Z and *per se* and." It would have been confusing to say, "X, Y, Z, and." Rather, the students said, "...and *per se* and." *Per se* means 'by itself', so the students were essentially saying, "X, Y, Z and, by itself, 'and'." Over the years, that phrase ("and *per se* and") was slurred by English speakers to *ampersand*.

At the heart of all great relationships lies an '&'. The ampersand has the power to beautifully connect two things without diminishing the value of either one. There is tremendous power in partnership, togetherness and in close collaboration. The word *koinonia*, or "together", is one of the defining words of the book of Acts, signifying the mutual bond we have in Christ.

> *And all who believed were together...*
>
> *Acts 2:44 (ESV)*

We get to connect with one another as fellow believers and work together with one purpose. I love what it says in Hebrews 10:24-25:

> *Let us think of ways to motivate one another to acts of love and good works. And let us not neglect our meeting together, as some people do, but encourage one another, especially now that the day of his return is drawing near.*
>
> *Hebrews 10:24-25 (NLT)*

Another translation starts:

> *Let's see how inventive we can be in encouraging love and helping out.*
>
> *Hebrews 10:24 (MSG)*

Let's realise the power of '&' today.

9

Thoroughly Furnished

All scripture is given by inspiration of God, and is profitable for doctrine, for reproof, for correction, for instruction in righteousness: That the man of God may be perfect, thoroughly furnished unto all good works.

2 Timothy 3:16-17 (KJV)

*L*et me take you back to my childhood for a moment. Sultry summer days had a nautical theme as my father's pastime centred around boats. It all started on a relatively small scale with an ordinary open boat and a very small outboard motor, not to mention the two wooden oars as a backup. Basically, we hugged the shore and did not leave our comfort zone. However, during the following summer Dad traded this simple boat for a bigger one bedecked with a compact cabin and its own inboard engine. Eventually he traded this boat for a floating appliance completely decked out with every imaginable device. It had a huge motor alongside its own sails, sleeping quarters and galley, gadgets like a depth-finder, barometric readings from the weather station, its own radio, hydraulic anchor, chart navigation and autopilot. He finally had the boat of his dreams, decked with everything he needed.

Why did I share this with you? When Paul described what the Word of God does in our lives in 2 Timothy 3:17, he used a Greek word that described a well-decked boat. The phrase "thoroughly furnished" is from the Greek word *exartidzo*, which means 'to completely deck out' or 'to fully supply'.

Imagine a ship capable of braving the highest Beaufort wind scale reading and the stormiest of seas because it has been fully equipped, dressed in the finest of gadgets, or to use the words of the verse, "thoroughly furnished".

Paul used this word to tell us that we are not prepared to set sail in life until the Word of God has done its work in our hearts and souls. It not only makes us wise unto salvation but helps us navigate the paths of life. When we are thoroughly furnished in the Word, we can venture out from shore by faith and face the storms and elements. We can launch out into the deep and let down our nets for the catch.

The question is, *are you thoroughly furnished?*

10

Love Me; Love Me Not

To Him who [always] loves us and who [has once for all] freed us [or washed us] from our sins by His own blood (His sacrificial death) – and formed us into a kingdom [as His subjects], priests to His God and Father – to Him be the glory and the power and the majesty and the dominion forever and ever. Amen.

Revelation 1:5-6 (AMP)

*D*id you ever play the daisy game? I remember as an adolescent lying on the playing fields at school with my friends and engaging in this game to determine if a certain 'someone' loved me or not. Armed with an oxeye daisy I began speaking alternately the phrases "he loves me" and "he loves me not", while picking one petal off a flower for each phrase. The couplet was repeated until all of the petals were discarded; the phrase spoken on picking off the last petal supposedly represented whether the object of my affection loved me or not. The tension built until the last petal told all. If the answer turned out to be "he loves me not", we would throw away the faulty flower and try it again on a different daisy! Apparently, the game is of French origin and is called *Euffeuiller la Marguerite*. A variant is to play the game with "he loves me, he loves me a lot".

It occurred to me recently that some people play the daisy game with God. Ever wondered how much God loves you? Does He love me today? Will He love me tomorrow?

With God you can always say, "He loves me, He loves me, He loves me." As it says in Revelation 1:5, "To Him who *[always]* loves us..."[14] Have you started to grasp how wide and long and high and deep the love

---

[14] AMP (emphasis added)

of Christ is[15] and to know this love that surpasses knowledge? Drink deeply of His love every day.

---

[15] See Ephesians 3:17-19

11

Hey Jude

Now unto him that is able to keep you from falling, and to present you faultless before the presence of his glory with exceeding joy, to the only wise God our Saviour, be glory and majesty, dominion and power, both now and ever. Amen.

Jude :24-25 (KJV)

The book of Jude is apparently the least read and therefore least known part of the New Testament. The above verses are part of Jude's dynamic doxology, finishing on a high note of praise and a great assurance for the redeemed. We cannot afford to gloss over them.

Jude reminds us that we serve a God who "is able". This is no new idea exclusive to the writing of Jude. In fact the theme of God's ability permeates the Bible. For example:

And God is able to make all grace abound to you, so that in all things at all times, having all that you need, you will abound in every good work.

2 Corinthians 9:8 (BSB, emphasis added)

Now to him who is able to do immeasurably more than all we ask or imagine, according to his power that is at work within us...

Ephesians 3:20 (NIV, emphasis added)

That is why I am suffering as I am. Yet this is no cause for shame, because I know whom I have believed, and am convinced that he is able to guard what I have entrusted to him until that day.

2 Timothy 1:12 (NIV, emphasis added)

Therefore he is able to save completely those who come to God through him, because he always lives to intercede for them.

Hebrews 7:25 (NIV, emphasis added)

Jude reminds us that we serve a God who is able. He is able to keep you from falling. He is able to present you faultless.

He keeps you. The Greek word for "keep", *phulasso,* means 'to watch, to carry out the function as a military guard or sentinel; to keep one's eye upon someone that he might remain safe'. *Phulasso* was used to describe the shepherds "keeping watch over their flock by night"[16], whilst savage wolves sought to devour the helpless sheep. Peter echoes the same truth; he states, we are "kept by the power of God"[17]. The psalmist also stated:

The LORD is your keeper.

Psalm 121:5 (ESV)

He is able to keep you.

He is also able to "present you faultless before the presence of his glory..." In other words He is able to make us presentable. That word "faultless" means 'without blemish'. It comes from the vocabulary of sacrificing animals in worship. Under Jewish law, before an animal could be offered as a sacrifice it must be inspected and if any blemish was found it must be rejected as unfit for an offering to God. Thankfully we are redeemed "with the precious blood of Christ, a lamb without blemish or defect"[18].

Let us join with Jude as he concludes, "...to the only wise God our Saviour, be glory and majesty, dominion and power, both now and ever. Amen."

---

[16] Luke 2:8 (ESV)
[17] 1 Peter 1:5 (KJV)
[18] 1 Peter 1:19 (NIV)

12

I Will Carry You

Listen to me, ... you whom I have upheld since your birth, and have carried since you were born. Even to your old age and grey hairs I am he, I am he who will sustain you. I have made you and I will carry you; I will sustain you and I will rescue you.

Isaiah 46:3-4 (NIV)

id you notice the word "carry"? God says, "I will carry you." Isaiah 46:3-4 tells us that from the day we are born till we are old and grey, God will carry us. We can never get to an age where we don't need to be carried by God. God assures His people that He will carry them from the womb to the tomb. How comforting it is to know that our God cares for us before we are born, when we get old and each moment in between!

In the opening verses of chapter 46 Isaiah has just mentioned the idols which needed to be carried:

...their idols are borne by beasts of burden. The images that are carried about are burdensome...

Isaiah 46:1 (NIV)

By contrast, God is the One who does the carrying. In those times when you think you can't carry on, God carries you.

Exodus 19:4 tells us of how after many years of hardship and oppression, God brought the children of Israel out of Egypt by carrying them on eagles' wings.

You know how I carried you on eagles' wings and brought you to myself.

Exodus 19:4 (NLT)

In my Bible as a bookmark I have *Footprints in the Sand*. It is a beautiful poem reminding us that we are never ever alone, especially during our most trying times. God is always with us.

> *Across the sky flashed scenes from his life. For each scene he noticed two sets of footprints in the sand: one belonging to him, and the other to the Lord. When the last scene of his life flashed before him, he looked back at the footprints in the sand. He noticed that many times along the path of his life there was only one set of footprints. He also noticed that it happened at the very lowest and saddest times in his life. This really bothered him and he questioned the Lord about it: "Lord, you said that once I decided to follow you, you'd walk with me all the way. But I have noticed that during the most troublesome times in my life, there is only one set of footprints. I don't understand why when I needed you most you would leave me." The Lord replied: "My son, my precious child, I love you and I would never leave you. During your times of trial and suffering, when you see only one set of footprints, it was then that I carried you."*

Remember Deuteronomy 33:27:

> *...underneath are the everlasting arms.*

Deuteronomy 33:27 (NIV)

You are safe in His arms. Protected. Cherished. Secure.

13

100%

Now one of them, when he saw that he had been healed, turned back, glorifying God with a loud voice, and he fell on his face at His feet, giving thanks to Him. And he was a Samaritan. Then Jesus answered and said, "Were there not ten cleansed? But the nine – where are they?"

Luke 17:15-17 (NASB)

There are many statistics in the Bible. For example:

- 90% of the lepers were unthankful. 10% of the lepers gave thanks to God.
- 75% of the hearers were unfruitful. 25% responded to the Word of God and bore fruit.[19]
- 50% of the bridesmaids were unready for the Bridegroom's return. 50% had oil in the lamps and a ready supply.[20]
- 83.4% of the spies sent out to scout the land were unbelieving. 16.6% had faith and a can-do attitude.[21]
- 99% of the sheep were unperturbed in the sheepfold. 1% was lost but the Shepherd searched for the one that was astray.[22]
- 100% matter to God.

He wants all of us safe in the sheepfold and enjoying His pasture.
He wants all of us full of faith.
He wants all of us ready for His return.
He wants all of us fruitful, responsive to His Word.
He wants all of us thankful.

---

[19] Mark 4:1-20
[20] Matthew 25:1-13
[21] Numbers 13:1-33
[22] Luke 15:3-7

14

Bezalel the Builder

I have filled him with the Spirit of God in wisdom, in understanding, in knowledge, and in all kinds of craftsmanship.

Exodus 31:3 (NASB)

*B*ezalel isn't a common household name such as David or Joshua. However, he is one of the unsung heroes mentioned in the book of Exodus. His story is tucked away amid a lot of technical details concerning construction and woodwork. God had announced His intention to have the people of Israel build a sanctuary for Him:

...that I may dwell among them ... [in a] tabernacle.

Exodus 25:8-9 (BSB)

This was to be no simple, matter-of-fact building of a physical edifice. Rather, it is a description with the highest aesthetic detail and design. In Exodus 31:2-5 God says:

See, I have called by name Bezalel son of Uri, the son of Hur, of the tribe of Judah. And I have filled him with the Spirit of God, in wisdom and ability, in understanding and intelligence, and in knowledge, and in all kinds of craftsmanship, to devise skillful works, to work in gold, and in silver, and in bronze, and in cutting of stones for setting, and in carving of wood, to work in all kinds of craftsmanship.

Exodus 31:2-5 (AMP)

Bezalel's name is richly meaningful in its three Hebrew syllables: *be* = 'in'; *tzal* = 'shadow'; *el* = 'God'. Thus, his name means 'in the shadow of God'. As shade is considered a protection in the Bible, such as from the heat of the sun, it thus is a metaphor for 'in the protection of God'.

He who dwells in the secret place of the Most High shall abide under the shadow of the Almighty. I will say of the Lord, He is my refuge and my fortress; my God, in him I will trust.

Psalm 91:1-2 (KJV)

Look again at verse 3 in today's passage: "I have filled him with the Spirit of God…" All his skill and wisdom was given to him by God. Bezalel was an astonishingly accomplished artisan. He was a metalworker, jeweller, gem-cutter and woodworker. Exodus 35 adds that he was an engraver, designer, embroiderer and weaver, and performed "every inventive work"[23]. He was gifted for a specific purpose. We tend to think of someone being filled with the Spirit of God as a prophet or perhaps a leader in battle. Images of Elijah or Gideon or Moses himself come to mind. But here was a Spirit-empowered craftsman. He, his assistant Oholiab and a whole bunch of apprentices built both the Tabernacle and the Ark of the Covenant, the holiest items in Israel's inventory.

God always equips those He calls. Just like with Bezalel, Oholiab and all the workers, the Holy Spirit will fill you and fit you for service so that you are empowered to serve well and dispense God's grace to others.

Each one should use whatever gift he has received to serve others, faithfully administering God's grace in its various forms.

1 Peter 4:10

It is God alone who gives us "wisdom and ability", "understanding and intelligence", "knowledge", "craftsmanship" etc. God has not only prepared specific works for you to do, but He also created you with the specific gifts necessary to do those good works. Now all that is needed is obedience. How could God use you to strengthen and build up the body of Christ?

---

[23] Exodus 35:33 (NASB)

15

Learn from Me

Whatever you have learned or received or heard from me, or seen in me – put it into practice. And the God of peace will be with you.

Philippians 4:9 (NIV)

We all have a preferential way in which we absorb, process, comprehend and retain information. Our learning styles usually fall into one of three 'categories': visual learners, auditory learners and kinaesthetic learners. Usually one of these styles is dominant. Around 30% of the population is made up of auditory learners, who learn best through hearing. An auditory-dominant learner prefers listening to what is being presented. They often talk to themselves. They also may move their lips and read out loud. Approximately 65% of the population are visual learners. Visual learners have two sub-channels: linguistic and spatial. Learners who are visual-linguistic like to learn through written language, such as reading and writing tasks. Learners who are visual-spatial usually do better with charts, demonstrations, videos and other visual materials. Kinaesthetic learners are a complex bunch and make up just 5% of the population. Kinaesthetic learners do best while touching and moving. When listening to lectures they may want to take notes for the sake of moving their hands. They typically use colour highlighters and take notes by drawing pictures, diagrams or doodling. They prefer a 'hands-on' approach.

Jesus says:

> *"Take my yoke upon you and learn from me, for I am gentle and humble in heart, and you will find rest for your souls."*
>
> *Matthew 11:29 (NIV)*

He says to us, "Learn from Me." We are invited to enter into a learning relationship with Him. Mary, in Luke 10:39, was praised because she was seated at the Lord's feet, listening to His Word. She was learning from Him in an auditory fashion. Those who are visual learners can learn of Him and from Him through the written words of the Bible. Those with a kinaesthetic leaning can learn by observing the pattern of godly examples, just as Paul taught in today's reading.

Let me share with you the beautiful words of R. A. Bertram:

> *In the great galleries of art that are the glory of London, Paris, Munich, Dresden, and Rome you may see the artists of the future. Young men toil there day after day, patiently copying the masterpieces of the painters who are world-renowned, learning thus to become painters themselves. Every line, every colour, every gradation of light and shade they put forth their utmost skill to imitate. They are not content that their picture should be something like the original; their ambition is to make their copy so exact that none but an experienced eye shall be able to tell which is the original and which is the copy. To-day, my friend, place yourself before the Lord Jesus; look on His character, so majestic in its righteousness, so tender and attractive in its love, and resolve to become like Him. Let not your ambition be lower than that with which the young artist sits down before some masterpiece of Raphael or Rubens, nor the patience with which you strive to accomplish it less.[24]*

---

[24] *Biblical Illustrator Commentary* Volume 4 (Matthew-John); edited by Joseph Samuel Exell; Delmarva Publications. (In this quote Exell is commenting on Matthew 11:29.)

16

Dark Adaptation

For ye were sometime in darkness, but now are ye light in the Lord; walk as children of light. ... And have no fellowship with the unfruitful works of darkness, but rather reprove them. For it is a shame even to speak of those things which are done of them in secret.

Ephesians 5:8,11-12 (KJV)

*I*f we go from the outdoors on a bright sunny day into a darkened cinema or a very dimly lit room, we are hardly able to see our surroundings at first. As time goes by, however, we gradually become able to detect the room's contents. Before long, we can see without difficulty and chuckle at the next person who clumsily stumbles and fumbles for a seat. This phenomenon is known as 'dark adaptation', and it typically takes between twenty and thirty minutes to reach its maximum, depending on the intensity of light exposure in the previous surroundings.

We Christians are often in the same predicament. We live in a dimly lit world, where sin is the rule and not the exception. Yet we are really children of the light.[25] We must always be on our guard that we do not become so accustomed to the darkness of our world that we think it is normal and conform to its dubious guidelines. The dim moral and spiritual insight of the world is not the standard that the Christian is to walk by.

You groped your way through that murk once, but no longer. You're out in the open now. The bright light of Christ makes your way plain. So no more stumbling around. Get on with it! The good, the right, the true – these are the actions

---

[25] See Ephesians 5:8

appropriate for daylight hours. Figure out what will please Christ, and then do it.

Ephesians 5:8-10 (MSG)

Paul told us:

...be not conformed to this world: but be ye transformed by the renewing of your mind...

Romans 12:2 (KJV)

The Message Bible puts it:

Don't become so well-adjusted to your culture that you fit into it without even thinking. Instead, fix your attention on God. You'll be changed from the inside out.

Romans 12:2 (MSG)

There's no room for dark adaptation here. Rather we should let our light shine.

Before the colonialists imposed national boundaries on Laos and Vietnam, the kings of Laos and Vietnam reached an agreement on taxation in the border areas. The deal was that those who ate short-grain rice, built their houses on stilts and decorated them with Indian-style serpents were considered Laotians. On the other hand, those who ate long-grain rice, built their houses on the ground and decorated them with Chinese-style dragons were considered Vietnamese. The exact location of a person's home wasn't what determined his or her nationality. Instead, each person belonged to the kingdom whose cultural values he or she exhibited. So it is with us; we live in the world, but as part of God's Kingdom we're to live according to the values of His Kingdom. Remember what Peter wrote:

But you are a chosen people, a royal priesthood, a holy nation, God's special possession, that you may declare the praises of him who called you out of darkness into his wonderful light.

1 Peter 2:9 (NIV)

Do you subscribe to the secular values of this world or the spiritual values of God's Kingdom?

17

Organise Your Prayer Life

I will remember the deeds of the LORD;
 yes, I will remember your miracles of long ago.
I will consider all your works
 and meditate on all your mighty deeds.

Psalm 77:11-12 (NIV)

o you want to be more intentional with your prayer life? A great way is to start a prayer journal. Sometimes we are prone to suffer from spiritual amnesia where we forget how faithfully God has answered our prayers. Instead of pausing to thank Him and celebrate the answer, we have taken it for granted and moved on to our next petition.

When Joshua and the Israelites came out from wandering the desert, God caused the Jordan River to part so they could pass over. Joshua called together twelve men – one from each of the tribes of Israel.

He told them, "Go into the middle of the Jordan, in front of the Ark of the Lord your God. Each of you must pick up one stone and carry it out on your shoulder – twelve stones in all, one for each of the twelve tribes of Israel. We will use these stones to build a memorial. In the future, your children will ask you, 'What do these stones mean?' Then you can tell them, 'They remind us that the Jordan River stopped flowing when the Ark of the Lord's Covenant went across.' These stones will stand as a memorial among the people of Israel forever."

Joshua 4:5-7 (NLT)

Keeping a prayer journal is a similar kind of reminder of how God has been good to you. Read and reread the jottings of your spiritual journey and you will be greatly encouraged. There's so much that happens in a lifetime and sometimes amid the flurry of activity we forget about the goodness and faithfulness of God. The prayer journal serves not only as a recounting of God's gracious ordaining in your life but also as a way of strengthening your faith when you face trials ahead. Through my simple prayer journal (an A4, hard-backed, spiral-bound notebook) I can trace and track God's faithful hand across the years of my life. He has truly been my Benefactor.

> *...you are he who took me from my mother's womb and you have been my benefactor from that day. My praise is continually of you.*
>
> *Psalm 71:6 (ESV)*

Not only am I praising Him for the past; I am trusting Him for this day and what lies ahead.

David's faith was strengthened against Goliath when he remembered the killing of the lion and bear. So it is with us: our faith is renewed when we read back over our journals and reflect on God's deliverance.

> *David said, "The LORD that delivered me out of the paw of the lion, and out of the paw of the bear, He will deliver me out of the hand of this Philistine."*
>
> *1 Samuel 17:37 (NASB)*

Start writing out your prayer requests with specificity. Remember to go back and write in your journal how God answered your prayer in His perfect timing. Then look back over the years and appreciate His goodness. As you remember His mighty deeds and consider all His works, may you be thankful and testify to His greatness.

18

Well Heeled

Instruct those who are rich in this present world not to be conceited or to fix their hope on the uncertainty of riches, but on God, who richly supplies us with all things to enjoy.

1 Timothy 6:17 (NASB)

*W*omen's shoes come in a wide array of heel heights. Apart from a pair of scuffed trainers for exercising and funky rabbit slippers for lounging at home, I am not a fan of flat shoes. I'm happiest in heels – from the tall and precarious stiletto embellished with dainty bows to the high platform heel on my chunky books. According to the latest stats, however, skyscrapers are no longer the height of fashion: flat shoes outsell heels by 148%. Research also reveals that higher heels substantially increase risk of foot soreness, blisters, bunions, falls, ankle sprains, plantar fasciitis, ingrown toenails, nerve damage in the feet and legs, and knee and back pain. Yet my Achilles heel is this: I still love my high shoes.

Have you heard of the term 'well-heeled'? It means to have plenty of money and its origin has to do with shoes; a person who has nice shoes is well-heeled and hence well-off. A person with good heels on his shoes seems to be in better circumstances than someone who's been in dire straits for a while and whose heels have worn down. That said, most if not all of us are amply clad when it comes to footwear and would thus be considered well-heeled.

Paul says to the 'well-heeled':

Command those who are rich in this present age not to be haughty, nor to trust in uncertain riches but in the living God, who gives us richly all things to enjoy. <u>Let them do good</u>, that they be rich in good works, ready to give, willing to share, storing up for themselves a good foundation for the time to come, that they may lay hold on eternal life.

1 Timothy 6:17-19 (NKJV, emphasis added)

Firstly, we should not set our hope in uncertain riches but in God who richly furnishes us with all things to enjoy.

And you shall remember the LORD your God, for it is He who gives you power to get wealth.

Deuteronomy 8:18 (NKJV)

We celebrate the Giver and put our trust in Him. Henry Parsons Crowell, founder of Quaker Oats, is a wonderful example of this. He died in 1943 at the age of eighty-two, having given away much of his income for over forty years. It seemed that the more money he gave, the more he prospered. He funded many Christian initiatives and became one of the wealthiest businessmen in Chicago at that time.

Secondly, we are to be rich in helping others, to be extravagantly generous in good works, open-handed and willing to share. There is a single Greek word tucked into verse 18, *eumetadotos,* which means 'ready to distribute'. There's more contentment in helping than in hoarding. We often measure generosity by the wrong standard. George Mueller said it well when he noted that God judges what we give by what we keep.

Matthew 10:8 is a good reminder:

Freely you have received, freely give.

Matthew 10:8 (NKJV)

19

Four Words of Defeat

We went to the land to which you sent us and, oh! It does flow with milk and honey! Just look at this fruit! The only thing is that the people who live there are fierce, their cities are huge and well fortified. Worse yet, we saw descendants of the giant Anak. Amalekites are spread out in the Negev; Hittites, Jebusites, and Amorites hold the hill country; and the Canaanites are established on the Mediterranean Sea and along the Jordan.

Numbers 13:27-29 (MSG)

They were on a reconnaissance mission to spy out the Promised Land. Who promised the land to them? God! If He promised the land to them, then they could certainly possess it. However, the ten spies spoke out four words which eventually brought them defeat. What were the words? *"The only thing is..."* They said, "It does flow with milk and honey! Just look at this fruit! *The only thing is* that the people who live there are fierce..."

In Numbers 13 and 14 we have three main groups:

- the ten spies with the negative report;
- the congregation who believed the negative report;
- Joshua and Caleb whose report differed.

When we read God's promises, which category do we fall into?

Are we like the ten spies who implied God's Word was null and void? We hear the words of Scripture but fall short of applying them to ourselves. We inject "the only thing is" into the promise and cannot believe it is applicable to our lives today. In fact, the Hebrew word *efes* (translated as "the only thing is") means, 'It's over!' So these ten spies nullified God's Word completely. They brought a potent cocktail of truth, lies and exaggeration.

Are we comparable to the congregation who sided with the negative report rather than the truth of God's Word? Negative attitudes cloud our judgement. They were on the threshold of the Promised Land but believed that their enemy was formidable, and resented the adversity in their lives. It is so important that we do not process the wrong data as we stand on the brink of victory.

Or have we the attitude of Joshua and Caleb?

"Let's go up and take the land – now. We can do it"

Numbers 13:30 (MSG)

In Numbers 14 they said:

"The land we travelled through and explored is a wonderful land! And if the Lord is pleased with us, he will bring us safely into that land and give it to us. It is a rich land flowing with milk and honey. Do not rebel against the Lord, and don't be afraid of the people of the land. They are only helpless prey to us! They have no protection, but the Lord is with us! Don't be afraid of them!"

Numbers 14:7-9 (NLT)

They didn't underestimate the military power of Canaan. But they did not underestimate God's power either. They trusted God against all odds. It took great courage to stand against the tide of unbelief.

Let's eradicate "the only thing is" from our thoughts and vocabulary. Let's side with God's truth and speak victory over our lives.

20

Are Your Burdens Heavy?

Cast your burden on the LORD,
And He shall sustain you...

Psalm 55:22 (NKJV)

*M*any of the bridges I cross have signs which indicate the 'load limit'. These signs show how much weight the bridge can bear. The structural engineers have determined the exact amount of stress the bridge can safely endure, knowing that too much strain can cause severe damage or complete collapse. Life in general can load us down. I don't know what burdens you are carrying. I don't know what is weighing you down and straining you. But I know what will lighten your load. Meditate on the following Scriptures today and allow God to lift each weight from your shoulders.

He says to you:

Pile your troubles on GOD's shoulders –
he'll carry your load, he'll help you out.

Psalm 55:22 (MSG)

God is prepared to carry your burdens and give you the daily sustenance you need. Our part is simply to cast our burdens on Him.

He says to you:

"Come to Me, all you who labor and are heavy laden, and I will give you rest. Take My yoke upon you and learn from Me, for I am gentle and lowly in heart, and you will find rest for your souls. For My yoke is easy and My burden is light."

Matthew 11:28-30 (NKJV)

Jesus will remove your heavy burden of guilt and hopelessness and give you true rest in Him.

He says to you:

Is this not the fast that I have chosen:

To loose the bonds of wickedness,
To undo the heavy burdens,
To let the oppressed go free,
And that you break every yoke?

Isaiah 58:6 (NKJV)

It's not God's desire that anyone should be oppressed with excessive burdens; allow Him to free you today and break every enslaving yoke.

He says to you:

You can throw the whole weight of your anxieties upon him,
for you are his personal concern.

1 Peter 5:7 (JBP)

Knowing that your heavenly Father is concerned about you personally can make any load seem lighter.

He says to you:

Even to your old age I am He, and even to your advanced old
age I will carry you! I have made you, and I will carry you; be
assured I will carry you and I will save you.

Isaiah 46:4 (AMP, emphasis added)

The Lord assures you that He is willing to continually uphold you throughout your life, with the intention of saving you eternally. He declares both His ability and His willingness to be your strength and support – mentally, emotionally and spiritually.

He says to you:

Lay aside every weight, and the sin which doth so easily beset
us…

Hebrews 12:1 (KJV)

When you do this you can then "run with endurance the race God has set before us"[26]. So take off the extra weight and run your race. Identify your burdens – worry, guilt, fear, grief, etc. – and allow the Lord to lighten your load.

---

[26] Hebrews 12:1 (KJV)

21

A Sound of the Abundance of Rain

Ask ye of the Lord rain in the time of the latter rain.

Zechariah 10:1 (KJV)

*I*n the UK, we talk incessantly about the weather. In a recent study, 94% of British people admitted to having talked about the weather in the past six hours and 38% in the last hour. Weather is a perfect icebreaker and our doorway into deeper conversation. Let's face it, we have a lot of weather! The range of vocabulary for rain alone demonstrates the breadth and diversity of linguistic options. It might be 'chucking it down', 'bucketing', 'pouring', 'lashing', 'spitting', 'raining cats and dogs' or 'raining stair-rods'. It might be muzzle or drizzle, a shower or a deluge, a soaking or a downpour. Perhaps the most graphic of the terms comes from French – a phrase which says simply it's 'raining like a cow relieving itself', which conjures an unpalatable but graphic image of force and abundance.

In Zechariah 10:1 we are instructed to ask for rain! One of the primary scriptures prayed throughout the revival pages of history is this particular verse. Throughout Scripture, rain has had a prophetic significance. There is something about water that speaks of the Spirit of God, and rain signifies an outpouring of living water. God says in Isaiah:

> *For I will pour water upon him who is thirsty,*
> *And floods on the dry ground.*
> *I will pour My Spirit upon your descendants,*
> *And My blessing upon your offspring.*
> *They will spring up among the grass*
> *Like willows or poplars by the watercourses.*
>
> *Isaiah 44:3-4 (NKJV)*

> *He will pour water on the thirsty.*
> *Rain down, you Heavens, from above,*
> *And let the skies pour down righteousness;*

Let the earth open, let salvation spring up,
And let righteousness grow with it.

Isaiah 45:8 (NKJV)

In 1 Kings 18 Elijah prayed fervently for rain until he saw a cloud the size of a man's hand. It grew into storm clouds and "there was a great rain"[27]. Before it ever appeared, Elijah said, "...there is the sound of abundance of rain."[28] If you looked around at this point, you would find a cloudless sky. It didn't sound like rain, it didn't feel like rain, it didn't smell like rain; yet the prophet said he could hear the rain! James summarises it this way:

The effective prayer of a righteous man can accomplish much.
Elijah was a man with a nature like ours, and he prayed
earnestly that it would not rain, and it did not rain on the earth
for three years and six months. Then he prayed again, and the
sky poured rain and the earth produced its fruit.

James 5:16-18 (NASB)

Notice he calls him a man "with a nature like ours". We must remember prayer is about ordinary people calling on an Omnipotent God. Like Elijah, are we willing to travail in prayer until revival showers are poured out over our nation again?

O that You would rend the heavens and come down!

---

[27] 1 Kings 18:45 (ESV)
[28] 1 Kings 18:41 (NKJV)

22

Under the Weather

Why are you cast down, O my inner self? And why should you moan over me and be disquieted within me? Hope in God and wait expectantly for Him, for I shall yet praise Him, my Help and my God.

Psalm 42:5 (AMPC)

As I pulled back my curtains at 5:45am one morning I was greeted with a spectacular scene. I looked out over the valley and saw a blanket of mysterious mist. I observed the ghostly grey hue of scattered houses under its heaviness but above the mist the sun was shining in its brilliance.

As I stood at the window, I was reminded that many people live their lives in a nebulous mist and cannot see beyond it. They are without hope. They allow troubles to cloud their vision and dampen their spirit. Anxious thoughts roll in unexpectedly and obscure the brightness of life. From my vantage point I knew that the obscuring haze was only temporary and would vanish within a short time. The disc of sun would be shining again on those houses. It was all about perspective.

Yet how often I lose perspective and panic. How often I have allowed circumstances to dampen my spirit.

Arise [from the depression and prostration in which circumstances have kept you – rise to a new life], shine [be radiant with the glory of the LORD];
For your light has come!
And the glory of the LORD is risen upon you!

Isaiah 60:1 (NKJV)

Don't live under the circumstances or under the weather. Look up and see God's perspective. As the Psalmist phrases it:

Hope in God and wait expectantly for Him, for I shall yet praise Him, my Help and my God.

Psalm 42:5 (AMPC)

23

Auto-Correct

For the word of God is living and active and sharper than any two-edged sword, and piercing as far as the division of soul and spirit, of both joints and marrow, and able to judge the thoughts and intentions of the heart.

Hebrews 4:12 (NASB)

With the advent of full touchscreen phones, companies like Apple and Google have developed advanced predictive text software, colloquially known as auto-correct, so that people spend less time typing. The aim is to make typing a smoother and speedier experience, but often it gets it wrong. Occasionally, auto-correct inadvertently morphs your note into an offensive message. Here is an example of autocorrect gone badly:

Hi, I need a haircut. Do you have anything Friday afternoon or Sat?

No idiot I'm booked out. Sorry

It's supposed to say NO I DON'T

NOT IDIOT sorry! auto correct!

Another one,

Happy birthday to you. Happy birthday to you. Happy birthday, dead husband. Happy birthday to you.

Thanks, I assume you meant "dear".

A teacher, wishing to encourage her student on her excellent essay, sent off a message, but unfortunately the message she received was:

Your essay is excrement!

I also was wrongly auto-corrected this week but thankfully I noticed it and was able to rectify it in time. I was texting about how we can trust

God's Word because it is the "inerrant" Word of God. However, autocorrect had changed the word "inerrant" to "inert"! Inert means powerless, inactive, impotent, ineffectual; it is really what the secular world want us to believe about the Bible: it is powerless to change our lives. It is often downplayed in favour of manmade philosophies. Yet the truth is encapsulated vividly in Hebrews 4:12 which reminds us that God's Word is living and active, alive and full power. The Amplified Bible puts it:

> For the Word that God speaks is alive and full of power [making it active, operative, energising, and effective].
>
> *Hebrews 4:12 (AMP)*

The Greek word for "active"is *energe* from which we get our word energy. It is energising and effective! Not inert!

Satan implanted four simple words in Eve's mind: "Did God really say?" His strategy hasn't changed as he seeks to get us to doubt and depart from God's Word by questioning His creation, His character and His promises. Jesus likened the Word of God to seed in His parable of the sower in Matthew 13. Seed, like the Bible, is not dead, but living, and it has the ability to bring forth more life abundantly. It is powerful to convict; powerful to convert; powerful to transform our lives. The Word of our Lord is efficacious for our salvation and sanctification. He told that we do not live by bread alone but by every word that proceeds from the mouth of God.[29] Bibles have been burned, Christians who translated the Bible have been martyred and Bible smugglers have been jailed. The Bible has been attacked by critics and scorned by intellectuals, but still it shows its power. May it be effective in our lives.

---

[29] See Matthew 4:4

24

The Snail Without a Shell

How long will you lie there, O sluggard? When will you arise from your sleep? A little sleep, a little slumber, a little folding of the hands to rest, and poverty will come upon you like a robber, and want like an armed man.

Proverbs 6:9-11 (ESV)

*S*lugs... Even the name gives me the creeps. If you wish to dream up an alien species for the next big sci-fi blockbuster, check out the slug's anatomy. They have no backbone but have tentacles, blowholes and twenty-seven thousand teeth! A slug is essentially a snail without a shell. Only 5% of the slug population is above ground at any one time. The other 95% is underground digesting your seedlings, laying eggs and feeding on roots and seed sprouts. A stalwart representative of the 5% population made his way into our home last year leaving his overnight trail of silvery slime secretions. After multiple attempts of following the telltale goo I met our resident slug, not of the normal bluish-black hue but a bilious-looking creature, the colour and texture of phlegm and copious with slime.

In the Bible there is a word which receives bad press and is derived from the word slug: it is the word "sluggard". A sluggard is someone who is habitually indolent or inactive, disinclined to work or exertion. The book of Proverbs goes to great lengths to describe 'Mr Slug'. In each case, the Bible shows how to spot a sluggard and warns of the consequences of being one.

Solomon asks some hard questions. "How long will you lie there? ... When will you arise from your sleep?" Applied today it could mean, "Why do you sit still and waste hours on end surfing the Internet? Why do you watch so much TV? Why do you manufacture excuses for inactivity? Why do you procrastinate from doing something positive?" Being a sluggard is the result of gradual lifestyle choices. Notice it is a *little* slumber, a *little* sleep, a *little* folding of the hands. By inches and minutes, his opportunity slips away.

Indulgence in laziness and idleness is contrary to our design as humans and contrary to our calling as Christians. Solomon offers advice saying:

> *Go to the ant, O sluggard; consider her ways, and be wise ... she prepares her bread in summer and gathers her food in harvest.*
>
> *Proverbs 6:6 (ESV)*

Have you ever watched an ant farm? We have only to watch the ant for a few minutes and we can see that it is industrious. It will not even hesitate if you block its path, finding some other way to accomplish its goals. The ant is a study in diligence. In Ecclesiastes Solomon instructs us:

> *Whatsoever thy hand findeth to do, do it with thy might.*
>
> *Ecclesiastes 9:10 (KJV)*

Throw yourself diligently into it. As believers we have a special reason and a special purpose to be diligent because the Bible says:

> *Whatever you do, work at it with all your heart, as working for the Lord...*
>
> *Colossians 3:23 (NIV)*

25

Go Bananas

...until we all reach unity in the faith and in the knowledge of the Son of God and become mature, attaining to the whole measure of the fullness of Christ.

Ephesians 4:13 (NIV)

The banana is a staple of fruit bowls across the country. The scientific name for banana is *musa sapientum*, which means 'fruit of the wise men'. The word 'banana' comes from the Arabic word *banan*, meaning 'finger'. A cluster of bananas is called a 'hand'. The banana is a nutritional powerhouse, an excellent source of potassium and vitamin B6, fibre and carbohydrate, and supplies some vitamin C. It come in its own handy, hygienic protective wrap and provides a quick-but-sustained energy boost.

How do you like your bananas? When would you consider them perfect for eating? A shade of light green? Perfectly yellow? With just a few brown spots? Or totally brown? It's funny; if you ask around, you'll find that everyone has a pretty strong opinion about their banana preferences. Apparently, a banana is considered fully ripe when it is yellow with brown spots on it. At this stage they are easily digestible and are powerful antioxidants.

What is your definition of maturity? Someone has defined maturity as:

> *...[being] able to carry money without spending it; to be able to bear an injustice without retaliating; to be able to keep on the job until it is finished; to be able to do one's duty even when one is not watched; and to be able to accept criticism without letting it whip you up.*[30]

The Bible speaks of us reaching spiritual maturity:

---

[30] Taken from *Success One Day at a Time;* John C. Maxwell; p.112

...let us press on to maturity...

Hebrews 6:1 (NASB)

When the New Testament addresses spiritual maturity, it uses the common Greek word *teleios* which means 'perfect' or 'complete'. What are marks of a person who is growing in spiritual maturity? A mature Christian is a believer whose life begins to take on the character of Christ-likeness. Paul speaks of a time when...

...we will no longer be infants, tossed back and forth by the waves, and blown here and there by every wind of teaching and by the cunning and craftiness of men in their deceitful scheming

Ephesians 4:14 (NIV)

Instead, we will speak the truth in love, growing in every way more and more like Christ.

Ephesians 4:15 (NLT)

Colossians 4:12 contains a snapshot of the prayer life of Epaphras:

[He is] always striving for you earnestly in his prayers, [pleading] that you may [as persons of ripe character and clear conviction] stand firm and mature [in spiritual growth], convinced and fully assured in everything willed by God.

Colossians 4:12 (AMP)

May the words "persons of ripe character and clear conviction" define our lives. May we press on to maturity and be marked by Christlike character and conduct.

26

Fragrant, Not Flagrant

We Christians have the unmistakeable "scent" of Christ, discernible alike to those who are being saved and to those who are heading for death. To the latter it seems like the very smell of doom, to the former it has the fresh fragrance of life itself.

2 Corinthians 2:14-15 (JBP)

Making a perfume is an elusive and complicated exercise in chemistry, creativity and commandeering our olfactory instinct. Naming a perfume is a no less demanding exercise. Ever wonder how perfumes got their names? Take, for example, my Mum's signature scent – Chanel No.5. It got its iconic name when Coco Chanel was presented with ten samples and selected the one labelled "No. 5". Imagine you were asked to name a new perfume or aftershave. What would you call it? Perhaps you would go for clever wordplay or appeal to its floral context. Check out the market and you will discover there are weird and intriguing names, such as Demeter (known for their unusual names) who came up with 'Funeral Home' and 'Lobster Scent'. If you want to smell like dinner, there's one for you called exactly that: 'Dinner'. I will stick with my favourite, 'La Vie est Belle' meaning 'Life is beautiful'.

The Bible tells us we are a fragrance of Christ. When we walk with God, we leave behind a sweet fragrance that can inspire others to follow.

Now He uses us to spread the knowledge of Christ everywhere, like a sweet perfume. Our lives are a Christ-like fragrance rising up to God. But this fragrance is perceived differently by those who are being saved and by those who are perishing. To those who are perishing, we are a dreadful smell of death and doom. But to those who are being saved, we are a life-giving perfume.

2 Corinthians 2:14-16 (NLT)

The Greek word translated as "fragrance" is *some*. It is used of Jesus in Ephesians 5:2:

> *...walk in the way of love, just as Christ loved us and gave himself up for us as a fragrant offering and sacrifice to God.*
>
> *Ephesians 5:2 (NIV)*

Paul used the same word of the Philippians when they had very generously sent gifts to him through Epaphroditus saying:

> *They are a fragrant offering, an acceptable sacrifice, pleasing to God.*
>
> *Philippians 4:18 (NIV)*

When it comes to a fragrance or perfume, it doesn't do much good or accomplish its purpose if it is kept tightly closed in a bottle. The aroma needs to be released for its purpose to be fulfilled. When this happens, people will be drawn to us, not because of our beauty or our bubbly personalities, but because they can sense the presence of Jesus in our lives. Not everyone will respond positively to the fragrance; to some it will smell of death, to others it will be life-giving. Nevertheless, we continue to spread the knowledge of Him in every place in a way that is fragrant, not flagrant. As you spritz on your spray today, remember that you are fragrant follower of Jesus diffusing the knowledge of Him everywhere you go.

27

The Quality of Integrity

And David shepherded them with integrity of heart; with skilful hands he led them.

Psalm 78:72 (NIVUK)

*I*t does exactly what it says on the tin' was originally the strapline of an advertising slogan (for Ronseal wood varnish) in the United Kingdom, which entered the British vernacular and became a common idiomatic phrase. It colloquially means that the name of something is an accurate description of its qualities. It smacks of integrity. Many people today view integrity as an outdated idea which is either expendable or no longer applicable in an age of moral relativism. However, integrity is essential if we are going to become people who positively and powerfully impact others. Integrity stems from the Latin word *integer* which means whole and complete. It requires an inner sense of wholeness and consistency of character. Just as we would talk about a whole number (integer), so also we can talk about a whole person who is undivided. A person of integrity is the same person in private that he or she is in public. Integrity has to do with a sense of consistency between a person's inner values and attitudes and his outward words and actions. The more consistent we are, the higher the degree of integrity we possess.

A good biblical example of integrity is Daniel.[31] Daniel's values, words and actions were thoroughly consistent. It is also the characteristic that distinguishes the godly leadership of David, as seen in today's passage. David wrote:

I know, my God, that you test the heart and are pleased with integrity.

1 Chronicles 29:17 (NIV)

---

[31] See Daniel 5:13-17

A person with integrity knows what is important to God and consistently lives in light of what is important to Him. It involves more than living our values; it involves subscribing to God's values. The contrast to integrity is duplicity:

> *The integrity of the upright guides them, but the unfaithful are destroyed by their duplicity.*
>
> *Proverbs 11:3 (NIV)*

If people who know you were asked for five words that describe you, would integrity be one of them? What are you like when no one else is around? How do you treat others who can't benefit you? Are you the same person when you are with different people? Are you the same person in public as in private? Do you do what you say you are going to do? Do you do the right thing no matter what the circumstances? Are you a person of integrity?

28

Insight from a Swallow

Even the stork in the sky knows the seasons, and the dove, swallow and crane return in due time. But my people don't know the LORD's ways.

Jeremiah 8:7 (CEB)

*H*ave you ever marvelled at the mass gatherings of swallows in autumn and wondered where they are heading or why they undertake such an arduous journey not once, but twice a year? By early September, most swallows are preparing to migrate. They flutter about restlessly, and often gather on telegraph wires. Most leave the UK during September, with early broods of youngsters being the first to go. But a few stragglers may hang around into October. The return journey to South Africa takes about six weeks. They travel down through western France, across the Pyrenees, down eastern Spain into Morocco, before crossing the Sahara Desert and the Congo – finally reaching South Africa and Namibia. They migrate during daylight, flying at low altitude and covering about 320 km (two hundred miles) each day. At night they roost in huge flocks in reed-beds at traditional stopover spots. Studies have shown that many swallows remarkably return to the same nest each year and prefer to refurbish rather than rebuild. Construction takes a lot of effort, requiring an average of 1,300 trips to gather enough pellets of material, and so it's well worth returning to last year's nest rather than starting afresh, especially if you have just flown ten thousand kilometres!

Jeremiah makes use of the flight of migratory birds to teach a valuable lesson. The birds know where they are going. They know the way. But the prophet says that the people around him do not know the Lord's ways. How about us?

[Jesus said,] "You know the way to the place I'm going."
Thomas asked, "Lord, we don't know where you are going.
How can we know the way?"

Jesus answered, "I am the way, the truth, and the life."

John 14:4-6 (CEB)

Do we know "the Way"? Followers of Jesus Christ were simply known as people of the Way in Acts 9:2 and 24:14 because they submitted to Him and sought to live by his truth. Are we living by His ways and identified by our behaviour? There is a beautiful prayer which we can employ in Psalm 25:

Make me know Your ways, O LORD;
teach me Your paths."

Psalm 25:4 (ESV)

Again, in Psalm 86:

Teach me Your way, O LORD;
I will walk in Your truth;
Unite my heart to fear Your name.

Psalm 86:11 (NKJV)

Notice too that the swallow pops up again in Psalm 84:3:

Even the sparrow has found a home,
and the swallow a nest for herself,
where she may have her young –
a place near your altar,
LORD Almighty, my King and my God.

Psalm 84:3 (NIV)

Do we have a similar desire to be in God's presence and base our home there? May a simple bird weighing only twenty grams be a visual reminder to us to know the Way, walk in the ways and dwell in His presence.

29

Our Most Valuable Non-Renewable Resource

This is the day the LORD has made.
We will rejoice and be glad in it.

Psalm 118:24 (NLT)

*A*re you squandering your most precious non-renewable resource? You may drive a fuel-efficient car, fit a catalytic converter, recycle your glass bottles, buy into biomass and do your best to conserve water. But you may be unaware that there is a resource, one that is entirely finite and disappearing at a consistent rate, which is wasted far too often. It is called time. Every day, every living person is provided with the same amount of time. Each day consists of eight-four thousand heartbeats, 1,440 minutes, 86,400 seconds to invest, a gift of twenty-four unexplored hours. We can't recoup the wasted time of yesterday but we can resolve to use today for the glory of God.

We all know today's Bible verse as it is often quoted. There is even a children's song which uses the verse as a refrain. But do we follow its advice? Do we rejoice in every day that God has given us?

We should see each day as a gift from God. Sometimes it is all too easy to fall into the trap of focussing lingeringly on the 'good old days' which have passed or fretting about the future, and in the process we forget to appreciate the present: today. There is wisdom in the Psalmist's approach. If we can neither change the past nor control the future, then it is pointless to give a lot of mental energy to either. The only thing that we can do is to make today count.

We need to rejoice in the present. We have to realise that this truly is the day that the Lord has made. We need to accept this day as a gift from God. *This* is the *day* the *Lord* has made. So what are we doing with our 'time'? Are we frittering it away, letting it slip through our fingers, squandering it in wanton waste?

So, then, be careful how you live. Do not be unwise but wise, making the best use of your time.

Ephesians 5:15-17 (ISV)

Behave wisely toward outsiders, making the best use of your time.

Colossians 4:5 (ISV)

We must assume responsibility for the use of our time. The Amplified Bible translates Ephesians 5:15-16 as:

Look carefully then how you walk! Live purposefully and worthily and accurately, not as the unwise and witless, but as wise (sensible, intelligent people), making the very most of the time [buying up each opportunity], because the days are evil.

Ephesians 5:15-17 (AMP)

Live purposefully and worthily and accurately. We all can take our days on this earth for granted. We can look at the day ahead just as something to get through rather than something to be glad about. But remember, every day is a gift from God. We should use our time to its best advantage, investing it wisely and productively. We should use it worthily in God-honouring ways, making it our goal to please to God in all we do. Today is not an accident and it is not incidental. God wants to be in the midst of this day with us. He wants to help us make it the best day that it can be. At the close of today, review the way in which you have spent your time. Ask yourself, did I make good use of my time; did I rejoice in it?

30

Portrait Painting

Because of His grace He made us right in His sight.

Titus 3:7 (NLT)

*H*ave you ever tried to paint someone's portrait? Back in art class at school a fellow pupil would be chosen as a 'sitter' and the rest of us had to sketch and paint their likeness. We were told to hold our pencils at arm's length, close one eye, measure the relative sizes against the length of the pencil and transfer the measurements to paper. We all looked professional as we held out our pencils but in reality, none of us had a clue!

Portraits are an effective way of telling us something about the person. A good portrait is not just a visual representation of a person; it will also reveal something about the essence of the person. Sometimes it can be cleverly implied through a certain facial expression or pose, setting, clothing or the artist's use of colour. An artist might choose to depict a person exactly as they are, warts and all; every pimple or scar is clearly memorialised in paint for all to see. Artists may sometimes even exaggerate a person's characteristics, good or bad, to make a caricature of them. Conversely, an artist might kindly overlook the person's flaws, correcting imperfections and presenting an idealised view of them.

The Queen sits for four portraits every year but not everyone sets out to flatter the monarchy and the paintings don't always go to plan. Lucian Freud was a well-respected British painter whose portraits weren't necessarily known to flatter; rather, they presented a stark naturalism that was often heavy with expression and folds and severe shading. The Queen sat for Freud in 2000. The portrait he gave her was both small and unflattering. Critics commented on his work as everything from "extremely unflattering" *(Daily Telegraph)*, "a travesty" *(The Sun)*, to "painful, brave, honest, stoical and, above all, clear-sighted" *(The Times)*.

There is a hunger in us all for realism, until, of course, we see the picture which was drawn or painted of us, and then we think it doesn't do us justice! The Bible paints a realistic picture of mankind. It gives us the good, the bad and the ugly with makind's propensity for every kind of evil. It includes descriptors we would rather gloss over or edit out. Paul tells us:

> *...there is none who does good, there is not even one.*
>
> *Romans 3:12 (NASB)*

> *...all have sinned and fall short of the glory of God.*
>
> *Romans 3:23 (NIV)*

But it also shows the surpassing riches of God's grace![32] The old hymn says it beautifully:

> *Grace, grace, God's grace;*
> *Grace that is greater than all my sin.*

When we come to Christ as broken sinners, He exchanges our sin nature for His righteousness. When God looks at us, He no longer sees our sin; He sees Jesus at work in our lives.

> *For by one sacrifice he has made perfect forever those who are being made holy.*
>
> *Hebrews 10:14 (NIV)*

Did you hear that: "made perfect forever"? In His eyes you are not a "travesty" but a treasure. You are His masterpiece, valuable and made acceptable.

---

[32] See Ephesians 2:7

September

October

October

1

Let Us

Let us go right into the presence of God with sincere hearts fully trusting him.

Hebrews 10:22 (NLT)

"**L**et us" is a common exhortation in the book of Hebrews. Here are a few other examples to ponder and practise:

- "Let us draw near with confidence to the throne of grace, so that we may receive mercy and find grace to help in time of need." (4:16, NASB)
- "Let us hold unswervingly to the hope we profess, for he who promised is faithful." (10:23, NIVUK)
- "…let us consider how we may spur one another on toward love and good deeds." (10:24, NIV)
- "…let us lay aside every weight…" (12:1, NKJV)
- "…let us run with endurance the race that is set before us…" (12:1b, NKJV)
- "…let us continually offer to God a sacrifice of praise – the fruit of lips that openly profess His name." (13:15, NIVUK)

All of these "let us" statements are possible because of our relationship with Jesus. We can draw near with confidence to the throne of grace because Jesus is our great High Priest who is touched with the feeling of our infirmities. We can draw near with a sincere heart and in full assurance of faith entering the Most Holy Place because of the blood of Jesus. We can hold unswervingly to the hope we profess because Jesus is faithful. We can spur one another on toward love and good deeds because Jesus is our motivation and the Day is approaching. We can lay aside the weights and run our race fixing our eyes on Jesus because He is the Pioneer and Perfecter of our faith. We can offer the sacrifice of praise through Jesus. Let us celebrate *Him!*

2

Power, Love and a Sound Mind

For God hath not given us the spirit of fear; but of power, and of love, and of a sound mind.

2 Timothy 1:7 (KJV)

I love this verse! It is such a powerful, comforting promise from our loving heavenly Father. Paul declares in the most plain and positive manner, "God hath not given us the spirit of fear." If you were to read it in the original Greek, you would see that the word "not" (*ou*) means 'absolutely not'. In other words, don't even entertain that thought! Vine's Expository Dictionary defines the Greek word *deilia*, which is translated here as "fear", as denoting "cowardice and timidity" and is never used in a good sense. Most of us recognise that dread, fright and terror are not from God, but we often fail to put things like timidity, shyness and cowardice in the same category. How do we overcome?

He has given us power. The Greek word for power is *dunamis*. Loosely, the word refers to 'strength, power, or ability'. It is the root word of our English words 'dynamite', 'dynamo' and 'dynamic'. In Matthew 22:29 Jesus tells the Sadducees:

> *'You are in error because you do not know the Scriptures or the power of God.'*

Matthew 22:29 (NIVUK)

Jesus told the disciples:

> *"But you shall receive power [dunamis] (ability, efficiency and might) when the Holy Spirit has come upon you; and you shall be My witnesses in Jerusalem and all Judea and Samaria and to the ends (the very bounds) of the earth."*

Acts 1:8 (AMPC)

He has given us love. The Greek word for love is *agape* and refers to the same love God has for us. Love is a very important concept in our walk with Christ.

> *There is no fear in love [dread does not exist], but full-grown (complete, perfect) love turns fear out of doors and expels every trace of terror!*
>
> *1 John 4:18 (AMPC)*

He has given us a sound mind. Sophronismos is the unique Greek word used to describe a "sound mind". Paul encourages his Colossian readers to...

> *...Set your minds on things above, not on earthly things.*
>
> *Colossians 3:2 (NIV)*

Make a conscious effort to fill your mind with God's Word and focus on Him.

> *Thou wilt keep him in perfect peace, whose mind is stayed on thee: because he trusteth in thee.*
>
> *Isaiah 26:3 (KJV)*

As you venture out today, remember that God has not given you a spirit of fear. Rather He wants you to step out in His power, assured of His love and possessing a sound mind.

3

Katharos

Blessed are the pure in heart,
For they shall see God.

Matthew 5:8 (NKJV)

*T*he sixth beatitude focusses on the pure in heart. The Greek word for pure is *katharos* and it is a fascinating word with a rich variety of applications, all of which have something to add to the meaning of this beatitude for the Christian life. For example:

- It can refer to cleanliness and could, for instance, be used of dirty clothes which have been washed clean and are free from adhesion to anything that soils. Think of washing detergent adverts.
- It can refer to corn which has been winnowed and cleansed of all chaff. It is tossed into the air against the wind which blows the chaff away.
- It can be used to denote that something has not been watered down and remains unmixed.
- It can be used of a ring which is pure gold and has not been alloyed with any other metal.
- It can refer to an army which has been purified and purged of all cowardly and undisciplined soldiers until there are only first-class fighting men left.

In a sentence, it refers to a heart which is cleansed, winnowed, unalloyed, sifted and purged. No wonder the psalmist prayed:

God, I invite your searching gaze into my heart.
Examine me through and through;
find out everything that may be hidden within me.
Put me to the test and sift through all my anxious cares.

Psalm 139:23 (TPT)

What a prayer!

Interestingly, the verb form of the word *katharos* is *katharizo* and it is found in 1 John 1:9. Here is the assurance it gives:

> *If we confess our sins, He is faithful and righteous to forgive us our sins and to cleanse us from all unrighteousness.*
>
> *1 John 1:9 (NKJV)*

4

Gait Analysis

So I, the prisoner for the Lord, appeal to you to live a life worthy of the calling to which you have been called [that is, to live a life that exhibits godly character, moral courage, personal integrity, and mature behaviour – a life that expresses gratitude to God for your salvation].

Ephesians 4:1 (AMP)

Buried under many sheets of paper I found an old appointment card for "Gait Analysis". Gait analysis is a method for identifying biomechanical abnormalities in the gait cycle – in other words, it's a means of assessing the way in which you walk. It is used to assess and treat individuals with conditions affecting their ability to walk and help athletes run more efficiently, identifying posture-related or movement-related problems in people with injuries. The client is asked walk for a few minutes on a treadmill while a recording is made of the feet. This footage is then slowed down and analysed in detail by a professional.

The book of Ephesians has a lot to say about 'gait analysis', or the way we walk. The Christian 'walk' or lifestyle has been described in several different ways. The Greek verb *peripateo* rendered "walk" (see verse below) refers to our daily Christian lifestyle. The Christian is to walk in a way that is dramatically different from his walk as an unbeliever.

...you must no longer walk as the Gentiles do, in the futility of their minds.

Ephesians 4:17 (ESV)

We must realise that there is a great chasm between the course of Christianity and the course of this world. When we follow the course of this world, we are off course. The Christian's outlook is different from that of the world. Our values are different, our goals are different and our philosophy of life is different.

Look carefully then how you walk, not as unwise but as wise.

Ephesians 5:15 (ESV))

Looking carefully at our spiritual walk is considered "wise". The term "carefully" is an adverb that denotes accuracy and attentiveness. We need to pay careful attention to how we live our lives. Paul tells us:

Therefore I, the prisoner of the Lord, implore you to walk in a manner worthy of the calling with which you have been called.

Ephesians 4:1 (NASB)

Paul has shown that we are elected, redeemed, sealed, made alive and reconciled unto God. Therefore, we ought to walk worthy of these honourable appellations and in keeping with these wonderful truths.

Christians are further instructed in Ephesians to "walk in love, as Christ also has loved us" (5:2, NKJV); and, "Walk as children of light" (5:8, NKJV).

Gait analysis is about our personal and unique way of walking. Unless the underlying causes of our dysfunctional movement patterns are addressed, our patterns won't change, and thus the risk of injury won't improve. Likewise, we injure ourselves when we try to walk in a manner other than that which God has designed for us. Let's take time to analyse our spiritual gait. Are we walking as children of light? Are we walking in love? Are we walking worthy of the calling we have received? Let's no longer walk in a dysfunctional way but walk wisely, giving careful attention to every step.

5

S-T-R-E-T-C-H

Enlarge the place of your tent, and let the curtains of your habitations be stretched out; spare not; lengthen your cords and strengthen your stakes, for you will spread abroad to the right hand and to the left; and your offspring will possess the nations and make the desolate cities to be inhabited.

Isaiah 54:2-3 (AMPC)

The rubber band was patented on March 17th, 1845 by Stephen Perry. I'm so grateful because I love rubber bands. They are one of the greatest inventions ever! They are inexpensive, simple, practical and useful. They hold multiple objects together, act as a lid gripper and frequently act as a makeshift hairband. However, rubber bands are pretty useless unless they are stretched. They must be stretched to be effective. When they are extended beyond their standard form, they can hold things together and accomplish their purpose.

Let's think of that word S-T-R-E-T-C-H. Stretching requires us to get out of our small boxes, our small routines, our small thinking and our limited view of God. Caleb and Joshua saw a place of enlargement before them, but the rest shrunk back and stayed small instead of stretching their faith. God invites us to be active participants in the process. In Matthew 12 we meet a man with a withered hand who is in the synagogue. Jesus said to the man, "Stretch out your hand."[33] So he stretched it out and it was completely restored, just as sound as the other. *"Stretch out your hand"* – that was the very thing he could not do. We are told that the Greek word for "withered"[34] speaks of 'dry, shrunken, wasted'.

He stretched it out, and his hand was completely restored.

Matthew 3:5 (NIV)

---

[33] Matthew 12:13 (NKJV)
[34] Matthew 12:10 (NKJV)

Here's something I want you to pay attention to: he had to stretch out his hand in faith. There was no visible change until he stretched it out.

Likewise, Moses received the instruction:

> *"Raise your staff and stretch out your hand over the sea to divide the water so that the Israelites can go through the sea on dry ground."*
>
> *Exodus 14:16 (NIVUK)*

We are told in verse 21:

> *Then Moses stretched out his hand over the sea; and the LORD swept the sea back by a strong east wind all night and turned the sea into dry land, so the waters were divided.*
>
> *Exodus 14:21 (AMP)*

God will ask you to stretch too. The Bible is filled with stretching exercises. He is actually stretching us to be the person He created us to be. He is stretching us so that we will be whole and effective people. Don't resist the process. "Let the curtains of your habitations be stretched out" so that you can accommodate His plans and purposes.

6

With True Reverence

Conduct yourselves in fear during the time of your stay upon earth.

1 Peter 1:17 (NASB)

And if you call upon Him as [your] Father Who judges each one impartially according to what he does, [then] you should conduct yourselves with true reverence throughout the time of your temporary residence [on the earth, whether long or short].

1 Peter 1:17 (AMP)

everence is the attitude of the person who is always aware that he/she is in the presence of God. In chapter one of 1 Peter we are given three reasons for this true reverence.

Firstly we are reminded that we are sojourners in this world, literally 'someone who is just passing through a place'. We are "temporary residents"[35]. Our true citizenship is in heaven. Life is to be lived in the shadow of eternity. Secondly, we can call God 'Father', but the very God whom we call Father is also the One who judges with strict impartiality. There is a danger when we overemphasise God as Judge and fail to relate to Him as Father. But equally dangerous is the case when we over-familiarise ourselves with God as Father and fail to maintain reverence for Him as Judge. Thirdly, we need to appreciate the truth that Jesus bought us with His precious blood and we now live for the honour of His Name.

...knowing that you were not redeemed with perishable things like silver or gold from your futile way of life inherited from

---

[35] NLT

your forefathers, but with precious blood, as of a lamb unblemished and spotless, the blood of Christ.

1 Peter 1:18 (NASB)

Are we conducting ourselves "in fear" and "with true reverence"? The Pulpit Commentary says:

In fear does not mean in dread or in terror; that meaning is contradicted by the whole tenor of this Epistle, and by the very name of God in this verse, Father.

Fear is synonymous with 'piety' in Old Testament language, and might be rendered 'reverence', or better still by the less frequently used but fine Saxon word 'awe'. Psalm 33:8 associates fearing God with standing in great awe of Him:

Let all the earth fear the LORD;
Let all the inhabitants of the world stand in awe of Him.

Psalm 33:8 (NKJV)

The word "awe" relates to enormous respect and great wonder. Again in Psalm 145 we read the beautiful words:

I will exalt You, my God, O King, and [with gratitude and submissive wonder] I will bless Your name forever and ever. Every day I will bless You and lovingly praise You; yes, [with awe-inspired reverence] I will praise Your name forever and ever.

Psalm 145:1-2 (AMP)

Did you notice the words "submissive wonder" and "awe inspired reverence"? That's how we should live. The sad summation of mankind in Romans 3:18 was this:

There is no fear of God [and His awesome power] before their eyes.

Romans 3:18 (AMP)

Are we in awe of God? Are we amazed in His presence? Are we living with reverential fear and never-ending gratitude for the enormous price that was paid for our salvation?

7

Inside Knowledge

Search me, God, and know my heart; test me and know my anxious thoughts. See if there is any offensive way in me, and lead me in the way everlasting.

Psalm 139:23-24 (NIVUK)

August Benziger was one of the most sought-after portrait painters of his time. He was a nineteenth to twentieth century painter known for his paintings of world leaders and other notable people. He was born in Einsiedeln, Switzerland in 1867, studied art in Munich and Vienna, and eventually ended up in the United States in the late 1890s. It was there that he was given the privileged position of painting the White House portrait of the twenty-fifth President, William McKinley. Other artists had attempted this feat but produced lacklustre depictions with a bland funeral appearance. Benziger was given carte blanche to enter and leave the White House as he pleased so that he could study the President at all times and from every angle. The painting, when unveiled, was a remarkable likeness capturing his deep personality. McKinley exuded warmth and dignity and quiet strength, and it was a great success (now on show in the National Portrait Gallery). The First Lady remarked, "You're the first artist to catch the deep fire burning within the soul of my husband."

Imagine he could paint you today and capture your heart in a painting. Suppose that he could paint your visage in a way that conveyed what is really going on in your heart. How would the painting look? Jesus knows exactly what's going on deep within each one us. Peter said:

"You, Lord, know the hearts of all men."

Acts 1:24 (HCSB)

Matthew recorded:

And Jesus knowing their thoughts said, "Why are you thinking evil in your hearts?"

Matthew 9:4 (NASB)

He knows everything you've ever done, thought, spoken or contemplated, and everything you will do, speak, think or contemplate. There is no part of your being (your mind, will, intellect, conscience, thinking, emotions, actions, motives) that is concealed from His sight.

David was very much aware of this when he wrote Psalm 139.

O LORD, you have searched me and known me!
You know when I sit down and when I rise up;
*   you discern my thoughts from afar.*

Psalm 139:1-2 (ESV)

The word he employed for "search" literally means 'to pierce through'. We speak poetically of 'seeing right through someone', referring to our ability to discern the other person's intentions. With God it is truth as He sees every aspect of our being. Whether we find inside knowledge thrilling or threatening depends on how we conduct our everyday lives. The same word "search" also carries the idea of searching for treasure or precious metal. Have you ever seen someone panning for gold? They sift through the dirt very carefully to find that gold or precious gem.

You scrutinize my path and my lying down,
And are intimately acquainted with all my ways.

Psalm 139:3 (NASB)

Does it bother you, knowing that God knows your every move? David continues:

Even before there is a word on my tongue,
Behold, O LORD, You know it all.

Psalm 139:4 (ESV)

Nothing escapes His all-seeing eye. He concludes the Psalm with an openness to God:

Search me, O God, and know my heart;
Try me and know my anxious thoughts;
And see if there be any hurtful way in me,
And lead me in the everlasting way.

Psalm 139:23-24 (NASB)

This transparency shows that he wants to be free of anything that would mar his relationship with God and prevent him from reaching his potential before God.

8

Awesome from Every Angle

God-of-the-Angel-Armies, who is like you, powerful and faithful from every angle?

Psalm 89:5 (MSG)

*H*ave you ever noticed that there's always one person in the family who volunteers to take all the photographs? They're usually the same people who really hate having their photo taken. After all, who really enjoys the experience? Many people feel a genuine dread when the cameras come out, but having your picture taken is almost inevitable in life. At weddings, social functions, family get-togethers, business or holiday, eventually someone is going to take a snapshot of you. So how can we be photogenic? The Internet suggests a few ploys anyone can implement to look better when the shutter clicks. Apparently, it is vital that the photographer chooses the right angle. Make sure the camera is at least eye level – if not higher. This angle will highlight those gorgeous eyes and hide any less than flattering elements under the chin. If you stand or sit straight-on, the camera sees more of your body. Instead, angle your body forty-five degrees away from the camera, push your weight on to your back foot and occupy your hands.

As we see in today's verse, the Bible tells us of God's beauty and perfection from every angle. God is absolute perfection in all His character and in all His ways. All His actions are resplendent with justice and truth.

The LORD is righteous in all His ways,
Gracious in all His works.

Psalm 145:17 (NASB)

He is the Rock, His work is perfect;
For all His ways are justice,

A God of truth and without injustice;
Righteous and upright is He.

Deuteronomy 32:4 (NKJV)

He is good all the time. He is forever faithful. He is perfect in His power; perfect in knowledge. His will is perfect.[36] His Word is perfect.[37] His way is perfect.[38]

From time to time newspapers and magazine reveal celebrities caught on camera in close-ups and extreme close-ups showing up blemishes, blotches, bulges and the wrinkles of time. However, the closer we look at God through His Word, the more we delight in Him as we see His perfect attributes on display. It makes us want to declare:

Great is the LORD! He is most worthy of praise!
No one can measure His greatness.

Psalm 145:3 (NLT)

Or as Paul put it:

Oh, how great are God's riches and wisdom and knowledge!
How impossible it is for us to understand His decisions and
His ways!

Romans 11:33 (NLT)

David desired to get as close as possible to God:

One thing have I asked of the LORD,
that will I seek after:
that I may dwell in the house of the LORD
all the days of my life,
to gaze upon the beauty of the LORD
and to inquire in his temple.

Psalm 27:4 (ESV)

In Psalm 100 he states:

For God is sheer beauty,

---

[36] See Romans 12:2
[37] See Psalm 19:7
[38] See 2 Samuel 22:31

all-generous in love,
loyal always and ever.

Psalm 100:5 (MSG)

God is sheer beauty, awesome from every angle. May we take time to capture and be captivated by His amazing attributes. May we zoom in to see our superlative God and find in Him our unchangeable Rock and Refuge.

9

Ironing Out Our Differences

*I urge Euodia and Syntyche to iron out their differences and
make up. God doesn't want his children holding grudges.*

Philippians 4:2 (MSG)

*I*roning is not something relished by all. Some people are
determined ironers who have the stamina and skill to steam that
pile of clothes into submission, leaving nothing but neatly folded
stacks of laundry in their wake. Others opt for synthetic, wrinkle-free
fabrics such as polyester or simply state, "It's meant to be creased!"
Personally, I find ironing immensely therapeutic. To reduce a heap of
crumpled laundry to a smooth, orderly pile is strangely satisfying. My
mum jokes that I would even iron the ironing board before starting!
There is surely great satisfaction in gliding the iron over the material and
smoothing out all of the wrinkles. In fact, an idiom is derived from this:
'to iron something out', meaning 'to resolve difficulties'. Sadly, tensions
fray the fabric of society today and altercations and arguments arise. This
happened even in the early Church as we saw in today's reading.

Perhaps it began as a small argument, but it mushroomed into a rift
which not only affected the two women but began to hurt the entire
congregation. Paul's example tells us that when we identify a "Euodia"
and "Syntyche" in our midst, we must seek to foster reconciliation and
harmony between them for the sake of the overall health of our body.
Small squabbles are clearly no small matter to the Lord! Our
reconciliation with others is in response to being reconciled to God
through the death of Jesus Christ.

Jesus said:

*"Therefore, if you are offering your gift at the altar and there
remember that your brother or sister has something against
you, leave your gift there in front of the altar. First go and be
reconciled to them; then come and offer your gift."*

Matthew 5:23-24 (NIV)

God cares about our bickering. Scripture tells us that we are to "let all bitterness and wrath and anger and clamour and slander be put away from [us], along with all malice"[39]. In writing to the Corinthians, Paul told them:

> *Finally, brothers, rejoice. Aim for restoration, comfort one another, agree with one another, live in peace; and the God of love and peace will be with you.*
>
> 2 Corinthians 13:11 (ESVUK)

Perhaps there are people in your life with whom God is calling you to be reconciled. Would not today be a good day to set matters right with someone you know? Whatever it is, get it ironed out.

---

[39] Ephesians 4:31 (ESVUK)

10

Beat the Wall

By faith the walls of Jericho fell down, after they were compassed about seven days.

Hebrews 11:30 (KJV)

Ninja Warrior UK, the notoriously tough assault course based on Sasuke, the Japanese TV show, has been airing on Saturday nights. Hopeful competitors from all walks of life push themselves to their limits as they try to complete a gruelling course requiring a combination of strength, agility, speed and balance. Those who successfully manage to stay out of the water and reach the final obstacle must scale the 4.25-metre, almost vertical "warped wall". With only a short runway and a steeply curving wall it is one of the most daunting and formidable obstacles of the course. But as the crowd chants, "Beat the wall, beat the wall," some have scaled it and hit the buzzer at the top.

What obstacles are you currently facing that seem insurmountable? In Joshua 6 we read of Jericho, a formidable city with huge, thick walls. The Israelites find themselves in need of supernatural intervention yet again. Though they have seen God open the Jordan River on their behalf, they wonder how He will help them overcome the formidable walls of Jericho. Joshua and the people were given specific instructions which, from a worldly perspective, did not seem to amount to much in the way of a military strategy. How could marching around the wall of Jericho one time for six days and seven times on the seventh day ever bring down massive walls that were wide enough, according to the ancient historian Josephus, to accommodate driving two chariots side by side? *How is all this marching going to bring down a wall? What's the point of blowing trumpets? Shouldn't we plan a surprise attack and scale the walls instead?* They probably wondered if Joshua was hearing God as accurately as Moses had heard Him. Surely Joshua had missed a portion of God's instructions, right? Wrong. Following such a plan demanded faith and obedience. God assured them:

"See! I have given Jericho into your hand…"

Joshua 6:2 (NKJV)

Faith believes the promise of God and acts on that promise. God will execute what the Israelites implement. God's people must participate in the battle of Jericho by marching around the city, and as a result God will give them victory by bringing down the walls. By acting in faith, these massive walls will implode upon themselves without a bulldozer or a wrecking ball because God Himself will bring them down. We know that at the end of the seventh trip around the wall, on the seventh day, Joshua gave the command. The people shouted *before* the wall fell – not *after.* They shouted in faith, believing God had given them the city. Those high walls were no match for the Almighty.

Notice the words "by faith" and "after" in today's passage. As we face the seemingly unassailable walls in our lives, we need to learn to believe the Lord, take Him at His Word and trust His timing for our victories. God could have torn the walls down on the first day, but He didn't. Nor did He do so on the second day, or the third, fourth, fifth or sixth day. It was God's will for the walls to come down on the seventh day, after the people had compassed the city seven times. If Joshua and the people had decided at any point that they had a better plan, they would have failed. But as they walked by faith and were completely obedient, God brought the walls down with nothing more than a shout. God knows best!

11

Your Accent Gives You Away

After a little while, those standing there went up to Peter and said, "Surely you are one of them; your accent gives you away."

Matthew 26:73

*I*n the musical *My Fair Lady* the character Henry Higgins was a linguist who could tell the home address of a person simply by listening to them speak. It is very hard to hide one's accent. Throughout the UK we have a a complex mosaic of accents. Whether it's Cockney rhyming slang, Scouse accents in Liverpool, the Geordie accent in Tyneside, the unique colloquial phrases in Yorkshire, not to mention the Brummie, Glaswegian and Ulster-Scots accents, there is huge diversity in the linguistic map of the United Kingdom. Examining theories of language acquisition, a team explored how accents, be they a strong twang or simply subtle inflections, can play a role in defining both who we are and other people's perceptions of us. Accents define us the moment we meet others. They pass on information about our lives. Peter found this out after Jesus' arrest:

After a little while, those standing there went up to Peter and said, "Surely you are one of them; your accent gives you away."

Matthew 26:73 (NIVUK)

Peter, earlier at the Last Supper, had assured Jesus that he would never deny Him or fall away from Him, even if all the others were to fall away; even if, says Peter, "I have to die with you"[40]. But Jesus had said, "Truly I say to you that this *very* night, before a rooster crows, you will deny Me three times."[41]

---

[40] Mark 14:31 (NKJV)
[41] Matthew 26:38 (NASB)

Now Jesus has been arrested. Matthew 26:58 tells us:

But Peter followed him at a distance, right up to the courtyard of the high priest.

Matthew 26:58 (NIVUK)

Peter was trying to gather information as to what was happening to Jesus without getting too close. He was outside in the courtyard trying to blend in with the crowd and remain *incognito* when a servant girl came to him, saying:

"You also were with Jesus of Galilee."

Matthew 26:69 (NKJV)

He denied it. Then another servant saw him and said to those who were there:

"This fellow also was with Jesus of Nazareth."

Matthew 26:71 (NKJV)

Again, he denied with an oath:

"I do not know the Man!"

Matthew 26:71 (NKJV)

A little later he was sitting warming himself by the fire in the courtyard of the high priest. Some bystanders came over to Peter and said:

"You must be one of them; we can tell by your Galilean accent."

Matthew 26:73 (NLT)

He was now like a cornered animal and swore to them:

"I don't know the man!"

Matthew 26:74 (MSG)

...and immediately the rooster crowed.

Then Peter remembered the word Jesus had spoken: "Before the rooster crows, you will disown me three times." And he went outside and wept bitterly.

Matthew 26:75 (NIVUK)

What a painful moment.

Peter had an accent that identified him as a Galilean. His mouth got him into trouble as his accent was the last piece of evidence needed to prove his association with the accused. "Your accent gives you away." The Galileans stressed the guttural sounds and its provincialisms were readily detected. It differed from the polished dialect of Judaea and Jerusalem and marked Peter as a disciple of Jesus. Let's ask ourselves, does our language makes it evident that we are of His company? Does the way we speak and the words we speak reveal Christian character? Do others recognise that we have been with Jesus? Or are we following Him at a distance and denying Him when it suits?

> *Let us hold fast the confession of our hope without wavering,*
> *for He who promised is faithful.*
>
> *Hebrews 10:23 (NKJV)*

12

Even There

Whither shall I go from thy spirit? or whither shall I flee from thy presence? If I ascend up into heaven, thou art there: if I make my bed in hell, behold, thou art there. If I take the wings of the morning, and dwell in the uttermost parts of the sea; even there shall thy hand lead me, and thy right hand shall hold me.

Psalm 139:7-10 (KJV)

*V*erse 10 says, "...even there shall thy hand lead me, and thy right hand shall hold me." The words "even there" stood out when I read it. David postulates, "Whither shall I flee from thy presence?" and the answer is, "Nowhere."

"If I ascend up into heaven, thou art there," he said. The first Soviet cosmonauts irreverently joked that they didn't see God from their spaceship. But God saw them.

Can a man hide himself in secret places so that I cannot see him? declares the LORD. Do I not fill heaven and earth? declares the LORD.

Jeremiah 23:24 (ESV)

God does not have spatial dimensions. The Message Bible says:

If I flew on morning's wings to the far western horizon, You'd find me in a minute – you're already there waiting!

Psalm 139:9-10 (MSG)

I'm reminded of the biblical story of Jonah, a man who tried to run away from God. Commanded to preach God's Word to the worst of Israel's enemies, he caught the first boat heading in the opposite direction. The text says:

*...he paid his fare and went on board, to go with [the sailors]
to Tarshish, away from the presence of the LORD.*

Jonah 1:3 (NRSV)

Like fugitives, we may run, but we cannot ultimately hide from the
God who penetrates even the darkness with the gaze of His light. God
was ahead of Jonah – in the storm at sea, in the belly of the fish, even
when he was rather unceremoniously deposited out of the fish's mouth
back onto shore.

One day C. H. Spurgeon was walking through the English country-
side with a friend. As they strolled along, the evangelist noticed a barn
with a weather vane on its roof. At the top of the vane were these words:
God Is Love. Spurgeon remarked to his companion that he thought this
was a rather inappropriate place for such a message.

"Weathervanes are changeable," he said, "but God's love is
constant."

"I don't agree with you about those words, Charles," replied his
friend. "You misunderstood the meaning. That sign is indicating a truth:
Regardless of which way the wind blows, God is love."

Likewise, regardless of which way we travel, God is there.

Donald Macleod writes concerning God being with us.

*This idea pervades Scripture and is set forth in terms of
virtually every preposition human language has to offer. God
is with us (Matthew 28:20), around us (Psalm 34:7), in us
(John 14:17), in the midst of us (Psalm 46:5), behind us (Psalm
139:5), underneath us (Deuteronomy 33:27), near us (Psalm
148:14) and before us (John 10:4).[42]*

As a believer David finds great comfort in the fact that God's hand
will lead and hold onto him.

*...yea though I walk through the valley of the shadow of
death, I will fear no evil, for Thou art with me.*

Psalm 23:4 (KJV)

*The LORD is with me; I will not be afraid. What can man do
to me?*

Psalm 118:6 (NIVUK)

---

[42] Behold Your God, p.66

God is our refuge and strength, a very present help in trouble.

Psalm 46:1 (NASB)

That Psalm goes on to describe the worst possible circumstances: "though the earth should change and though the mountains slip into the heart of the sea"[43], God is "very present." No matter how tumultuous the situation, God is always there! If we would only realise that God is with us every moment of our lives, what a difference it would make; what a comfort we would find in that constant presence.

---

[43] Psalm 46:2 (NASB)

13

Eight Ways to Be More Effective

For if these things are yours and abound, you will be neither barren nor unfruitful in the knowledge of our Lord Jesus Christ. For he who lacks these things is shortsighted, even to blindness, and has forgotten that he was cleansed from his old sins.

2 Peter 1:8-9 (NKJV)

For if you possess these qualities in increasing measure, they will keep you from being ineffective and unproductive in your knowledge of our Lord Jesus Christ.

2 Peter 1:8-9 (NIVUK

"*I*f these things are yours" – *what* things? "If you possess these qualities" – which qualities? I want to know, don't you? Especially if they'll make us more effective and productive. These "things" or "qualities" refers back to verse 5 in which Peter lists eight qualities we should diligently add to our lives, eight ways to be more effective. He says:

For this very reason, make every effort to add to your faith goodness; and to goodness, knowledge; and to knowledge, self-control; and to self-control, perseverance; and to perseverance, godliness; and to godliness, mutual affection; and to mutual affection, love. For if you possess these qualities in increasing measure, they will keep you from being ineffective and unproductive in your knowledge of our Lord Jesus Christ. But whoever does not have them is nearsighted and blind, forgetting that they have been cleansed from their past sins.

2 Peter 1:5-9 (NIVUK

Verse 9 contains a clear and concise warning. Those who don't have these qualities in their lives are "nearsighted". The word used here (Greek *myopazo*) is the word we use for an eye condition called myopia. Myopia is an abnormal eye condition in which light rays from distant objects, passing through the lens, focus in front of the retina instead of on it. This causes blurry vision. The more common term for this problem is short-sightedness, a malady that affects millions of people. Thankfully, we have the knowledge and technology today to overcome this obstacle, allowing the physical problem to be corrected by eyeglasses, contact lenses and sometimes even surgery.

Spiritually speaking, Peter says there is a danger of being myopic in outlook. It is easy to become short-sighted in life, to see things only as they appear at the moment, and to be unable to take the long view of matters. Such people live in a fog, totally unaware of the urgency of the times. A Christian who lacks the qualities mentioned in verses 5 to 7 is short-sighted. We need to examine our vision constantly using Peter's list as a chart. Test the eyesight of your soul by this standard. See where you are weak and then strengthen that area of your Christian life. Notice the phrase "increasing measure". There is always room to grow and that's why we are supposed to apply all diligence to our walk with the Lord. God wants you to abound, to exceed in these spiritual qualities, so that you are never unproductive, ineffective or short-sighted.

14

Detonate the Land Mine of Fear

"I am leaving you with a gift – peace of mind and heart. And the peace I give is a gift the world cannot give. So don't be troubled or afraid."

John 14:27 (TLB)

Sylvester always ended up with a blackened body after stepping on the land mines or explosives planted by Tweety, but soon he was back in action. Cartoons are not meant to be realistic and it is certainly not a reflection of stepping on a land mine. Worldwide, there are thought to be some one hundred million land mines, many of which are leftover from conflicts long since finished. Every year these mines kill and maim thousands of people without mercy or discrimination, the vast majority of which are innocent civilians. I was reading recently of the potential of a drone which can autonomously map, detect and detonate land mines and could potentially clear the world of these deadly devices in less than ten years' time.

The enemy plants land mines of fear in our lives with the purpose "to steal, kill and destroy"[44]. He usually does this by planting thoughts into our minds; thoughts of impending disaster and defeat which play relentlessly over and over on the reel of our reasoning. It sneaks into our hearts without permission, painting a picture of helplessness and hopelessness. It steals our peace and concentration. The detonation of the land mine of fear depends on our reflection on the Word of God and having our minds renewed.

You will keep him in perfect peace,
Whose mind is stayed on you,
Because he trusts in you.

Isaiah 26:3 (NKJV)

---

[44] John 10:10 (TLB)

Jesus' words in today's verse tell us:

> *"Peace I leave with you; My [own] peace I now give and bequeath to you. Not as the world gives do I give to you. Do not let your hearts be troubled, neither let them be afraid. [Stop allowing yourselves to be agitated and disturbed; and do not permit yourselves to be fearful and intimidated and cowardly and unsettled.]"*
>
> *John 14:27 (AMPC)*

Jesus has given you peace! "Peace I leave with you." Interestingly, the word "leave" actually means 'bequeath', the way in which a rich man bequeaths his estate to his beneficiary. He reassures His disciples, urging them, "So don't be troubled or afraid." Jesus has a message for you today and it is the same: "Don't be afraid." Permit His words to abide in you today. Allow His voice of love to permeate your being and dissolve every last trace of fear. He says, "Stop allowing yourselves to be agitated and disturbed; and do not permit yourselves to be fearful and intimidated and cowardly and unsettled."

15

Say it With Flowers

And why are you worried about clothing? Observe how the lilies of the field grow; they do not toil nor do they spin, yet I say to you that not even Solomon in all his glory clothed himself like one of these. But if God so clothes the grass of the field, which is alive today and tomorrow is thrown into the furnace, will He not much more clothe you? You of little faith! Do not worry then...

Matthew 6:28-30 (NASB)

The Japanese call it *Hanakotoba. Hanakotoba* is the Japanese name for assigning meanings to flowers. Floriography – a sophisticated name for the language of flowers – was coined in the Victorian era and was used as a means of coded communication through various flowers and floral arrangements, allowing people to express feelings which otherwise could not be spoken. As the long list of flowers and their meanings grew, books containing the meanings of various plants and flowers (floriography dictionaries) were published. Some eight hundred flowers were given precise meanings. The red rose is the best known, as it has symbolised love and passion since time immemorial. However, choosing an orchid could cost you dearly. According to the language of flowers, an orchid can mean "you are the most precious person to me in the world", but also "my wealth is yours". For centuries people have been conveying messages of congratulations, celebration, love and condolences with fresh flowers. What better way to show appreciation and thought than with a bouquet of freshly cut flowers. A floral bouquet, no matter how simple or elaborate, is the one thing that brings a smile to many faces. The slogan 'Say it with flowers' was created a very long time ago, in 1917, by the Florists' Telegraph Delivery group (FTD).

Jesus had an important message to convey and He said it with flowers. To be precise, "lilies". The message was, and is, "Do not worry…"

Jesus uses the lily as an illustration. The principle runs through the vein: if we were to understand the raiment of a flower, and God's government over its intricacies, we would then understand the care of our Heavenly Father for His children as something infinitely more valuable. Have you ever thought about the parts of a flower and the intricacies of their design as a magnificent and wondrous spectacle of God's power and creative ability? In considering the lily (or any flower) we should pause to think about the Creator of the flower and His providence over our lives. We are clothed in a righteousness that no lily could ever claim. We are clothed with power from on high. All our needs have been, are, and shall be, provided by Him for His own glory. Jesus says it clearly with flowers: there is no need to worry.

16

Schrödinger's Cat

...the people that do know their God shall be strong, and do exploits.

Daniel 11:32 (KJV)

*E*rwin Schrödinger, the Austrian quantum physicist and Nobel Prize winner, is known for his thought experiment known as 'Schrödinger's Cat'. In the hypothetical experiment, which the physicist devised in 1935, an imaginary cat is placed in a sealed box for an hour. Also inside the box are a container of radioactive material, a Geiger counter (a simple machine that detects radioactive particles), a hammer and a vial of poison. There is a fifty-fifty chance that within one hour a single radioactive particle will be emitted. If the Geiger counter detects that the radioactive material has decayed, a mechanism is triggered, smashing the bottle of poison and killing the cat. If it doesn't, the flask is unbroken and the cat remains alive.

The point is that you would not know if the cat was dead or alive until you opened the box, so that until the box was opened, the cat was (in a sense) both dead *and* alive. Until we open the box, we don't know the result.

When we open our Bibles, we discover that we can 'know' certain truths with certainty. For example:

Be still, and know that I am God...

Psalm 46:10 (NKJV)

Biblically to "know" God is not to know *about* Him in an abstract and impersonal manner or solely with intellectual apprehension; but rather to enter into a personal, close relationship with Him. It is relational and real. The psalmist beckons us:

Know that the LORD is God.
It is He who made us, and we are His;

we are His people, the sheep of his pasture.

Psalm 100:3 (NIVUK)

Our Creator wants us to know Him. Isn't that amazing? It is one thing to *know about* someone, such as a celebrity footballer, and altogether another matter to actually *know* the footballer himself. You can watch every match, memorise every statistic, and amass every piece of memorabilia yet never really know the person himself. To truly know him you would have to enjoy a relationship with him. The biblical word translated here as "know" means to actually 'know God on an intimate level'. God spoke through the prophet Jeremiah:

"Let not the wise man glory in his wisdom,
Let not the mighty man glory in his might,
Nor let the rich man glory in his riches;
But let him who glories glory in this,
That he understands and knows Me."

Jeremiah 9:23-24 (NKJV)

Daniel declared:

"The people that do know their God shall be strong, and do exploits."

Daniel 11:32 (KJV)

Centuries before the birth of Christ, Job, the suffering patriarch of Uz, exclaimed:

"...I know that my Redeemer lives..."

Job 19:25 (NKJV)

Do *you* know Him?
Jesus said:

"I am the good shepherd; I know my sheep and my sheep know me."

John 10:14 (NIV)

He stated:

"Now this is eternal life: that they may know you, the only true God, and Jesus Christ, whom you have sent."

John 17:3 (NIVUK)

John put it:

I write these things to you who believe in the name of the Son of God, that you may know that you have eternal life.

1 John 5:13 (ESV)

You may *know* that you have eternal life. The Amplified Bible puts it:

...that you may know [with settled and absolute knowledge] that you [already] have life, yes, eternal life.

1 John 5:13 (AMP)

We can know the promise of eternal life here and now and experience the joy of knowing God on a daily basis. Thankfully, there is no room for surmising or speculation or supposition.

17

The Only Constant in Life

For I am the LORD, I change not...

Malachi 3:6 (KJV)

*I*t's amazing how much change can happen in a few decades. Someone shared with me a post about how food has changed since the 1950s. The following are a few examples. Pasta had not been invented. Curry was a surname. A takeaway was a mathematical problem. A Big Mac was what someone wore when it was raining. Fish didn't have fingers in those days. Eating raw fish was called poverty, not sushi. Prunes were medicinal. Surprisingly, muesli was readily available; it was called cattle feed. Water came out of the tap; if someone had suggested bottling it and charging more than petrol for it they would have become a laughing stock.

"Change is the only constant in life." This saying is attributed to the Greek philosopher Heraclitus. In making such a statement, Heraclitus captured what many others have also recognised, namely, that there is precious little that is stable in the world around us. The same philosopher illustrated the point about change being ever-present by saying, "No man ever steps into the same river twice." An ever-flowing river is there and even has a name, yet the water in it keeps changing so that from one second to the next, it is really a different river. In the midst of this ever-changing world, it's a real comfort to me to know that we have a never-changing God.

God is unchanging and constant. This is the attribute known as the immutability of God. Everything around us can appear to be changing and even spinning out of control. Yet God is stable, constant and never-changing. He's the Rock to which we constantly cling. He is the only security in which we can trust without reservation. There is absolutely no variation with Him, no eclipse of His loving kindness and care. The very name of God, "I Am", denotes His constancy. He is the One with whom "there is no variation or shadow of turning"[45]. Fickleness and betrayal characterise human nature, but stability and faithfulness are true of our God. His mood never changes. What a pleasure to know that whenever we approach Him through the merits of His Son, He receives us warmly and lovingly. He never gets tired of our coming to Him. In fact, He keeps inviting us to come. We can always count on Him. This gives us confidence in the midst of unsettling times. The greatest sense of security against the disorientation and disruption of change is our reliance on the unchanging God. Take some time today to meditate on the Lord's unchanging character.

---

[45] James 1:17 (KJV)

18

Why are Superheroes so Popular?

He is the one we proclaim, admonishing and teaching everyone with all wisdom, so that we may present everyone fully mature in Christ. To this end I strenuously contend with all the energy Christ so powerfully works in me.

Colossians 1:28-29 (NIV)

The recent influx of superhero hype confirms that superheroes are no longer confined to the comic book world. Thanks to the big screen, superheroes have never enjoyed greater visibility. For some, watching the movie isn't enough; they want to don their favourite character's costume (cosplaying). Why are they so popular? Is it because they stand up for the common man and rescue people? Is it simply an escapist fantasy? Are they aspirational figures? Experts tell us that people flock to see them because there is a part of all of us which thrills at the thought that somebody's ordinary life might suddenly be transformed into something extraordinary – that he or she, and even you and I, might secretly have within us, or suddenly be given, the gifts needed to do something super.

Look at how the Amplified Bible brings out the nuance of the words in today's passage:

...striving with all the superhuman energy which He so mightily enkindles and works within me.

Colossians 1:29 (AMP)

Superhuman energy! What an encouragement to the Christian. Paul calls it:

...his incomparably great power for us who believe.

Ephesians 1:19 (NIVUK)

We are energised by God's power. He is the Energiser! He "works". It is His energy working within us. In the original Greek, this reads more literally "the working [*energeia* = noun] of Him Who is working [*energeo* = verb] in me in power [*dunamis*]". Paul is energised by the supernatural power of Christ in Him.

Much of our anxiety in life comes from underestimating the implications of the power of God in our lives. If only we fully grasped its magnitude! If only our eyes were flooded with light to understand the surpassing greatness of His power in and for us who believe. We don't need to don a Superman cape because we are already clothed with power from on high. There is an extraordinary power available to you and me, a power that can accomplish far more than we ordinarily think or imagine.

> *Now unto Him that is able to do exceeding abundantly above all that we ask or think, according to the power that worketh in us...*
>
> *Ephesians 3:20 (KJV)*

Remember today you have superhuman energy for every task. You can do all things through Christ who strengthens you. Paul said:

> *I have strength for all things in Christ Who empowers me [I am ready for anything and equal to anything through Him Who infuses inner strength into me; I am self-sufficient in Christ's sufficiency].*
>
> *Philippians 4:13 (AMPC)*

19

Flourish

The [uncompromisingly] righteous shall flourish like the palm tree [be long-lived, stately, upright, useful, and fruitful]; they shall grow like a cedar in Lebanon [majestic, stable, durable, and incorruptible]. Planted in the house of the Lord, they shall flourish in the courts of our God. [Growing in grace] they shall still bring forth fruit in old age; they shall be full of sap [of spiritual vitality] and [rich in the] verdure [of trust, love, and contentment]. [They are living memorials] to show that the Lord is upright and faithful to His promises; He is my Rock, and there is no unrighteousness in Him.

Psalm 92:12-15 (AMP)

What does it mean to flourish 'like a palm tree'? In what respect does the palm tree flourish? What is there about the palm tree which would suggest its employment as a comparison to describe a righteous person? Let's consider its calibre. An amazing fact about the palm tree is that every part of it is useful. The palm leaves are used to cover homes and as material for fences. They are also useful for making baskets and other items. Even the seeds, when ground, produced food for camels. According to Encyclopaedia Britannica:

Palms are of the greatest economic importance. They furnish food, clothing, shelter, fuel, fibre, paper, starch, oil, sugar, wax, wine, tannin, dying materials, resin and a host of minor products...

The Syrians enumerated 360 different uses to which it may be put; and the Bible testifies that it still bears its fruit in old age. Apparently, as a palm tree grows older, its fruit grows sweeter. Its principle of growth is that it is an endogen and grows from within, a lovely reminder to us that we are transformed from inside as well as that our 'inner man' is renewed day by day.

The palm branch is a sign of victory. Palm leaves were thrown upon the ground in front of Jesus at the triumphal entry of Jesus into Jerusalem.[46] Revelation 7:9-15 pictures a huge group of overcoming people holding palm branches in their hands:

> *After this I saw a vast crowd, too great to count, from every nation and tribe and people and language, standing in front of the throne and before the Lamb. They were clothed in white robes and held palm branches in their hands.*
>
> *Revelation 7:9 (TLB)*

Palm trees are very resilient trees. They are almost hurricane-proof, because their genetic make-up allows them to be very flexible. The elasticity of the fibre of the palm will bend but not break. It has been well documented that during storms with hurricane force winds, the palm tree is seldom uprooted and destroyed. In fact, palm trees can bend down almost to ground level during a violent storm but will recover to their original position when the storm has passed. Also, scientists have found that when the storm is over and the palm tree stands upright again, the palm tree is actually stronger than it was before the storm.

It flourishes even in a desert and is unmoved by the scorching and withering blasts. The palm tree does not simply *grow* in the desert; it *flourishes*. It has extremely deep tap roots – called a root ball – and thus can flourish even in adverse conditions, growing tall and living long. A group of palm trees is an oasis offering a verdant canopy to weary pilgrims. Exodus 15 records:

> *After leaving Marah, the Israelites traveled on to the oasis of Elim, where they found twelve springs and seventy palm trees. They camped there beside the water.*
>
> *Exodus 15:27 (NLT)*

May we flourish like the palm tree and be useful, durable, overcoming and a source of refreshing and relief to others.

---

[46] See John 12:13

20

My Cup Overflows

You anoint my head with oil;
My cup overflows.

Psalm 23:5 (NKJV)

My cup overflows. Or, in the words of the King James Version (KJV), "my cup runneth over". The question, "Is the cup half-full or half-empty?" has for many years highlighted the tendency for two people to see the same situation in different ways. Some say, "I'm a cup-half-empty sort of person," meaning they see things from a pessimistic point of view; others say, "I'm a cup-half-full sort of person," meaning they are optimistic in outlook. My challenge is for each one of us to see ourselves as a "my cup overflows" sort of person, just like the Psalmist.

Jesus said:

I came that they might have life, and might have it abundantly.

John 10:10b (NKJV)

The word He uses for "abundantly" is *perissos*, meaning 'to have a surplus', 'beyond measure', 'superabundance', 'surplus', 'till it overflows'. The Amplified Bible puts it:

I came that they may have and enjoy life, and have it in abundance (to the full, till it overflows).

John 10:10b (AMP)

In Christ we can have overflowing joy, overflowing love and overflowing peace, etc. Our Father puts a 'super' on the natural, an 'extra' on the ordinary and an 'over' on the flowing. As John states:

For out of His fullness (abundance) we have all received [all had a share and we were all supplied with] one grace after another and spiritual blessing upon spiritual blessing and even favour upon favour and gift [heaped] upon gift.

John 1:16 (AMP)

Our Father is the One "who is able to do immeasurably more than all we ask or imagine"[47]. Therefore allow your cup to overflow to be a blessing to others, to abound in every good work and benefit the Kingdom of God. Overflow with grace because God has lavished His grace on us. Overflow with love because He has poured His love into us. Overflow with mercy because He has been rich in mercy towards us. Overflow with generosity because He has made us rich in every way. Overflow with blessing because He has blessed us with every spiritual blessing in Christ.

---

[47] Ephesians 3:20 (NIVUK)

21

We Are His

Know that the LORD, he is God!
It is he who made us, and we are his;
we are his people, and the sheep of his pasture.

Psalm 100:3 (ESV)

*I*t still retains its spot in my bookcase after many years and multiple readings to my children: *Six-Dinner Sid* by Inga Moore. Unbeknownst to each of his owners, Sid the conniving cat lives with six different people on the same street. Sid thus gets six different delicious meals each day, plenty of coveted attention and he responds to six different names. Each owner on Aristotle Street believes that Sid belongs only to them – until the day he is found out! Having developed a dreadful cough he is taken to the local vet not once but six times, which blows his cover! At the end of the book Sid moves on to friendlier Pythagoras Place and presumably continues his ploys.

Today I'm contemplating the subject of ownership, belonging and dependency. What a joy and delight it is to know that we belong to God. We are His, and He takes care of what belongs to Him. We are His people. According to today's verse, our part is to "know" this amazing actuality, to perceive this truth and allow it to sink in. "We are his" may be simply three short monosyllabic words but they speak volumes. All of our other roles in life must be seen in the light of this primary reality. First and foremost, *we are His*. We do not need to drink from the stagnant ponds of this world which can never quench our thirst or satisfy. God is our ever-flowing fountain of life and our dependency is on Him. In Isaiah 43 God tells us:

"Fear not, for I have redeemed you;
I have called you by name;
You are Mine."

Isaiah 43:1 (NKJV)

God tells us that there is no need to fear because we are His. "Fear not … You are Mine."

In the New Testament we are further reminded of these marvellous truths:

…we are His workmanship…

Ephesians 2:10 (NKJV)

You are not your own, for you were bought with a price.

1 Corinthians 6:19-20 (ESVUK)

See what kind of love the Father has given to us, that we should be called children of God; and so we are.

1 John 3:1 (ESVUK)

[God] set his seal of ownership on us, and put his Spirit in our hearts as a deposit, guaranteeing what is to come.

2 Corinthians 1:22 (NIVUK)

The reality is that everything we have and everything we do is a result of God's grace and a reflection that we are His. God calls his people to live in expectant and full dependency on Him, believing and trusting that what seems impossible to us is possible with God.

22

Tough as a Tardigrade

In conclusion, be strong in the Lord [be empowered through your union with Him]; draw your strength from Him [that strength which His boundless might provides].

Ephesians 6:10 (AMP)

I'm sure if you have ventured into your garden from time to time you have encountered a cockroach, traditionally looked upon as Earth's most resilient species. However the world's most indestructible creature is apparently the tardigrade. Tardigrades are tough and tiny (about one millimetre long). They have podgy scrunched-up faces with plump folds of flesh resembling puffer coats. They seem adept at living in some of the harshest regions of Earth. They have been discovered up the Himalayas, in Japanese hot springs, at the bottom of the ocean and in Antarctica. They can also survive radiation, boiling liquids, massive amounts of pressure and even the vacuum of space without any protection. In 2007, thousands of tardigrades were attached to a satellite and blasted into space. After the satellite had returned to Earth, scientists found that many had survived. In difficult conditions, they survive by going into an almost death-like state called cryptobiosis. They curl into a dehydrated ball, called a tun, by retracting their head and legs. They can remain motionless this way for decades. If reintroduced to water, the tardigrade can come back to life in just a few hours.

Jesus Christ told us that we would have tough times and adverse situations in life but we are well able to face them. We are encouraged to press on in whatever environment we find ourselves knowing that we are overcomers and can draw our supernatural strength from our relationship with Christ. Paul, who wrote today's verse, was empowered through his union with Christ. He drew his strength from Him day by day and that's why he could say:

We are troubled on every side, yet not distressed; we are perplexed, but not in despair; persecuted, but not forsaken; cast down, but not destroyed.

2 Corinthians 4:8-9 (KJV)

Paul told his protégé Timothy:

You ... must endure hardship as a good soldier of Jesus Christ.

2 Timothy 2:3 (NKJV)

We have at our disposal a vast source of power that is rarely tapped into to the fullest. "His boundless might" means that it is limitless; it is infinite! We can draw from this source. We can endure what comes our way.

23

Twenty-Four Feet

"Now that I, your Lord and Teacher, have washed your feet,
you also should wash one another's feet."

John 13:14 (NIVUK)

I love the beach but dislike the sand. Sound weird? It's fantastic to kick off the suffocating shoes, unreel the socks and freely stroll barefoot along a sandy beach. The downside is the amount of sand I carry home. It's abrasive, it's grainy, it's everywhere. Thankfully, nowadays there are beach showers and baby wipes to ease the discomfort. Walking in sandals on the dusty dirt tracks of Israel in the first century made it imperative that feet be washed before a communal meal, especially since people reclined at a low table and feet were very much in evidence. It was a common act of hospitality when a visitor came calling to provide him with water for the washing of his feet. In fact, washing the feet of weary travellers would have been a job delegated to a Gentile slave by the host.

The Gospel of John is the only Gospel to record the act of footwashing by Jesus. It happened in the upper room, just prior to the Last Supper. The basin was there, the towel was there and everything was ready. But no one moved in to wash the others' feet. When Jesus rose from the table and began to wash the feet of the disciples,[48] He was doing the work of the lowliest of servants. The disciples must have been stunned at this act of humility and condescension, that Christ, their Lord and master, should wash their feet. Jesus' attitude of servanthood was in direct contrast to that of the disciples, who had been arguing among themselves as to which of them was the greatest, recorded in Luke 22:24. Further, when Jesus washed the disciples' feet, He told them (and us):

---

[48] See John 13

"I have given you an example, that you should do as I have done to you."

John 13:15 (NKJV)

As His followers, we are to emulate Him, serving one another in lowliness of heart and mind. How timely is this lesson as we live in a very proud and egotistical generation where it is considered acceptable and even normal for people to promote themselves, to praise themselves and to put themselves first.

Notice that Jesus washed the feet of *all* the disciples, even Judas the betrayer. There were twenty-four feet. He didn't skip Judas when He got to Him. Jesus knew what was in Judas' heart. He knew the betrayal and the treacherous kiss was coming. Jesus knew the anguish that was ahead: the beatings, the scourging, the agonising walk to Golgotha and the ultimate death on the cross. Yet, even in this moment of humbling Himself, Jesus stooped and washed Judas' feet. In what were literally the last hours before His death, Jesus kept showing them His love over and over. Judas would betray him with clean feet.

It is amazing how much Jesus loved these men knowing that they had been arguing about who was the greatest and which one would sit at His right hand. He knew that they were about to forsake Him and flee for their lives. He knew that Peter would deny Him, Judas would betray Him and Thomas would doubt Him. Yet He loved them to the end. May we learn from His example, putting on the apron of humility and serving one another in love.

24

Beautiful Attitudes

And he opened his mouth, and taught them, saying,
Blessed are the poor in spirit: for theirs is the kingdom of
heaven.
Blessed are they that mourn: for they shall be comforted.
Blessed are the meek: for they shall inherit the earth.
Blessed are they which do hunger and thirst after
righteousness: for they shall be filled.
Blessed are the merciful: for they shall obtain mercy.
Blessed are the pure in heart: for they shall see God.
Blessed are the peacemakers: for they shall be called the
children of God.
Blessed are they which are persecuted for righteousness' sake:
for theirs is the kingdom of heaven.

Matthew 5:2-10 (KJV)

*H*ave you ever accidentally made up a word by merging two words together? The technical term for this is making 'portmanteau' words, i.e. words which combine the sounds and meanings of two others. Portmanteau is French for a case which opens into two equal sections. Examples of portmanteau words include: brunch (breakfast/lunch), glamping (glamour/camping); smog (smoke/fog); cineplex (cinema/complex); newscast (news/broadcast). Today's verses are taken from Jesus' teaching on the Sermon on the Mount in Matthew 5. This section is commonly referred to as The Beatitudes. I love how a little girl, when referring to The Beatitudes, said that it was short for The Beautiful Attitudes. Indeed, they are beautiful attitudes we should all display in our lives. The word 'beatitude' comes from the Latin word for 'blessed'. Jesus told us that we are blessed when we are:

- *poor in spirit, humble*
  The poor in spirit are not proud, arrogant or self-sufficient. They know they are weak, sinful and in need of God's grace.

- *penitent, mourn for our sin*
  This refers to sincere sorrow or grief because of sin and disobedience, causing repentance to God. Jesus gives rest to such mourners.[49]

- *poised/meek*
  One problem with the English word meek is that it rhymes with weak, and people have linked the two words together for years. However, the word Jesus used refers to strength under control.

- *passionate for righteousness, hungering and thirsting for it*
  Jesus said a little later, "...seek first the kingdom of God and his righteousness, and all these things will be added to you."[50]

- *pardoning, merciful*
  To receive mercy is to not receive what we really deserve. God grants mercy to us when He forgives our sins and saves us. He does not give us the punishment we deserve. Jesus calls for us to do the same for others.

- *pure in heart*
  A pure heart has no hypocrisy, no guile, no hidden motives. The Psalmist prayed, "Create in me a pure heart, O God, and renew a steadfast spirit within me."[51]

- *peacemakers, makers and maintainers of peace*
  We have been given a ministry of reconciliation. A peacemaker is one whose posture is primarily active, relentless in the pursuit of justice, harmony and reconciliation.

- *persecuted for righteousness*
  The Christian message is at odds with the world's mindset and so people will "mock you and persecute you and lie about you and say all sorts of evil things against you because you are my followers"[52].

May we take these beautiful attitudes and allow the contours of Christlike character to define our lives.

---

[49] See Matthew 11:28-30
[50] Matthew 6:33 (ESV)
[51] Psalm 51:10 (NIVUK)
[52] Matthew 5:11 (NLT)

25

Macro Skies and Micro Self

When I consider your heavens, the work of your fingers,
The moon and the stars, which you have set in place,
What is mankind that you are mindful of them,
Human beings that you care for them?

Psalm 8:3-4 (NKJV)

*T*he tenor of Psalm 8 is replete with doxology and reverence. The aim is that we stand in awe of God and worship Him. It begins and ends with the same noble words which frame the Psalm:

O, LORD, our Lord, how majestic is Your Name in all the earth.

Psalm 8:1 (ESV)

To be "majestic" refers to excellence, eminence and extravagance. It is equivalent to Your Majesty or Your Highness in the UK. God's name is majestic and it is to be magnified in all the earth. In verses 3 and 4, David describes God as the majestic Creator who makes stars with His fingers. He is saying that the seemingly infinite universe, the broad expanse of the sky, populated with innumerable stars, is the work of the fingers of God.

Abraham Lincoln wrote:

I never behold [the heavens filled with stars] that I do not feel I am looking in the face of God. I can see how it might be possible for a man to look down upon the earth and be an atheist, but I cannot conceive how he could look up into the heavens and say there is no God.

There's something about a clear night filled with a huge moon and bright shining stars that creates a sense of wonder in most people. Kepler, the astronomer, was troubled by one of his friends who denied the existence of God and took the view of the universe that it came into being of itself by mechanical methods. Kepler, in order to convince his friend, constructed a model of the sun with the planets circling round it.

When his friend came into the Observatory and saw the beautiful model, he exclaimed with delight, "How beautiful it is! Who made it?"

And Kepler carelessly answered, "No one made it. It made itself."

His friend looked at him and said, "Nonsense, tell me who made it."

Kepler then replied, "Friend, you say that this little toy could not make itself. It is but a very weak imitation of this great universe which, I understood, you believe did make itself."

We believe in the God of creation who flung the stars into the universe!

The Message Bible phrases verses 3 to 4:

> *I look up at your macro-skies, dark and enormous, your handmade sky-jewelry, moon and stars mounted in their settings. Then I look at my micro-self and wonder, why do you bother with us? Why take a second look our way?*
>
> Psalm 8:3-4 (MSG)

The rhetorical question of Psalm 8:4 emphasises that man is an insignificant creature in the universe. Yet God cares for him immensely. God's gracious concern for mankind in the universe should humble and amaze us. Let us be thankful that He is mindful of us and that He cares. Our fitting response is surely to exalt His name and live to serve His majesty.

> *O magnify the LORD with me,*
> *And let us exalt his name together.*
>
> Psalm 34:3 (NKJV)

> *Ascribe to the LORD the glory due his name.*
>
> Psalm 96:8 (ESV)

> *Bless the LORD, O my soul, and all that is within me, bless his holy name!*
>
> Psalm 103:1 (ESV)

26

Glorious Living

It's in Christ that we find out who we are and what we are living for. Long before we first heard of Christ and got our hopes up, he had his eye on us, had designs on us for glorious living, part of the overall purpose he is working out in everything and everyone.

Ephesians 1:11-12 (MSG)

The evangelist Billy Graham told the following story in January 2000 when addressing a group of leaders in Charlotte, North Carolina:

Einstein was once traveling from Princeton on a train when the conductor came down the aisle, punching the tickets of every passenger. When he came to Einstein, Einstein reached in his vest pocket. He couldn't find his ticket, so he reached in his trouser pockets. It wasn't there, so he looked in his briefcase but couldn't find it. Then he looked in the seat beside him. He still couldn't find it.

The conductor said, "Dr. Einstein, I know who you are. We all know who you are. I'm sure you bought a ticket. Don't worry about it."

Einstein nodded appreciatively.

The conductor continued down the aisle punching tickets. As he was ready to move to the next car, he turned around and saw the great physicist down on his hands and knees looking under his seat for his ticket.

The conductor rushed back and said, "Dr. Einstein, Dr. Einstein, don't worry, I know who you are. No problem. You don't need a ticket. I'm sure you bought one."

Einstein looked at him and said, "Young man, I too, know who I am. What I don't know is where I'm going."

Perhaps you can relate to Einstein in that metaphorically you cannot find your ticket and you have no idea where you are going. Or perhaps you could take this story one step further – unlike Einstein, perhaps you are not even sure who you are. Paul revealed in our verses today that it's in Christ that we find out who we are and what we are living for. Our identity, purpose and direction in life only make sense in relationship with Him. These are the great longings of the human heart. Paul stood up in the meeting of the Areopagus and said about Christ in Acts 17:28:

"...in Him we live and move and have our being..."

Acts 17:28 (NKJV)

Understanding who we are in Christ and our seating in Him will change the way we live and cause us to rise above adversity. Failing to understand our identity in Him will leave us helplessly fumbling our way in life, searching in the wrong places for meaning, and will keep us living far below our privileges. Ephesians 1:12 states that God has "designs on us for glorious living"[53]. How many of us can look at our lives and say that we are living gloriously? Any room for improvement? Then study all of Ephesians 1 and ask God to open the eyes of your heart, to know the hope of His calling and the riches of the glory of His inheritance in the saints.[54]

---

[53] Ephesians 1:12 (MSG)
[54] See Ephesians 1:18-19

27

Say What You See

Surely goodness and mercy shall follow me
All the days of my life;
And I will dwell in the house of the LORD
Forever.

Psalm 23:6 (NKJV)

*I*n Disney's heart-warming film *Christopher Robin*, Christopher as an adult is reunited with his friends from the Hundred Acre Wood. While I find each character charming in their own particular way, I have to admit that I have a soft spot for Eeyore, the dismal grey donkey. He wallows in misery a little bit, but he has this endearing melancholy to him. There's something poignantly oxymoronic about him — that such hilarity and joy can come from a gloomy character. In the film, Brad Garrett voices Eeyore. He's popped up before in films such as *A Bug's Life* (Dim), *Finding Nemo* (Bloat), *Ratatouille* (Gusteau), *Finding Dory* (Bloat), *Tangled* (Hook Hand Thug), *Planes* (Chug) and *The Country Bears* (Fred Bedderhead). In an interview he said, "I felt like I was kind of born to play Eeyore, because of the face and also my attitude to life, which is very Eeyore-ish." The dialogue in the film which I clearly remember centred around a game which Pooh like to play:

> *Winnie the Pooh: "It's called 'Say What You See'. You first, Eeyore."*
> *Eeyore: "Disgrace. Shame. Humiliation."*
> *Winnie the Pooh: "Well, that's one way to play it."*

How do we see life? Are there any aspects indicative of an 'Eeyore-ish' outlook? Or do we always look on the bright side of life?

Let's break down today's verse and say the words slowly.

Goodness. It speaks of God's beneficence, His beautiful benefits, favour and blessings. We have a good God and we are encouraged to taste and see that God is good.

Mercy. It speaks of the loyal, royal love of God and His unfailing kindness and compassion. It's His nature to be merciful and forgiving. Instead of justly condemning us when we err, He does not treat us as our sins deserve.

Follow. The actual Hebrew word means 'pursue, to set off after someone in order to catch him'. God's goodness and mercy do not follow a hundred metres behind us every day – they are pursuing us in order to catch us every day.

All the days of my life. All means all. His mercies are new every morning and continue all day long. Circumstances may be tough. Life situations may not be what we want. Some roads that stretch ahead are not what we would have chosen to travel, but we are assured of God's goodness and mercy every step of the way.

Say what you see. *Goodness. Mercy. Following me. All the days of my life.*

28

Valued, Not Invisible

But Jesus said, "Someone did touch Me, for I was aware that power had gone out of Me." When the woman saw that she had not escaped notice, she came trembling and fell down before Him, and declared in the presence of all the people the reason why she had touched Him, and how she had been immediately healed. And He said to her, "Daughter, your faith has made you well; go in peace."

Luke 8:46-48 (NASB)

The Invisible Mouse is a seven-minute animated cartoon of Tom and Jerry in which Tom chases Jerry into a bottle of invisible ink and Jerry then proceeds to have fun torturing him. Tom cannot see Jerry and is puzzled, especially when he hears the piano playing with no visible assistance and when Jerry procures a straw and drinks Tom's chocolate milk.

Being invisible, however, isn't always fun. There are people who have basically felt invisible their whole lives. You can feel invisible in your family, in a crowd, in your class at school, in your place of work, even in your marriage. No one seems to know – or care – that you're there. I read an excerpt from the Gospels which carries real hope for people who feel marginalised, ignored or passed over. It concerns a woman who had been battling an incurable condition for twelve years and had run out of hope. Mark tells us that she had spent all her money trying to get well but only got worse. Desperate, she pushed her way through the masses that were thronging around Jesus, believing she would be healed if she could just touch His robe. She pressed through the crowd, touched Him and was healed of her affliction.

But look particularly at what Jesus said in verse 46: "Someone touched me!"

"But Lord," Simon Peter interruptsed "everybody's touching You!"

"No, Simon," Jesus said, "*somebody touched me.*"

Jesus, who was being mobbed by people on every side, said "Somebody touched Me." Then we read the wonderful footnote to the story:

> *Then the woman, seeing that she could not go unnoticed ... fell at His feet."*
>
> *Luke 8:47 (NIVUK)*

Jesus said:

> *"Daughter, your faith has healed you. Go in peace."*
>
> *Luke 8:48 (NIVUK)*

Not only did Jesus notice her, He called her "daughter". This desperate woman discovered that day what millions have discovered since. Nobody goes unnoticed by Jesus. You are never invisible to Him. How *could* you be? The Bible says that each and every one of us was "created by Him and for Him"[55]. You are not just some random protoplasm wandering across this planet. You are created by Jesus as a divine original, created for a love relationship with God. He knows you. He loves you. He has plans for you.

Jesus tenderly reminds each one of us:

> *"Are not five sparrows sold for two pennies? And not one of them is forgotten before God. Why, even the hairs of your head are all numbered."*
>
> *Luke 12:6-7 (ESV)*

If God cares so much about these things that seem so insignificant to us, and not one of them is forgotten, how much more does He care for you? Then Jesus finishes by saying:

> *"Fear not; you are of more value than many sparrows!"*
>
> *Luke 12:8 (ESV)*

In God's eyes you matter. You are valued, not invisible.

---

[55] Colossians 1:16 (DARBY)

29

Ru-hoo Ru Ru-hoo

He put a new song in my mouth,
a song of praise to our God.
Many will see and fear,
and put their trust in the LORD.

Psalm 40:3 (ESV)

*A*re we distinctive by our song and the sound which comes from our mouths? One of my favourite birds weighs around 450g – the equivalent of more than forty blue tits. Its Latinate name is *Columba palumbus*, better known to us as the wood pigeon. It is a portly greyish bird with a white neck collar (absent in newly fledged young). It takes a young woody, also known as a squab, sixteen weeks to acquire its distinctive white neck ring. This big and burly bird is most distinctive for its cooing sound. It is somewhat distinct from other birds in the garden. In fact, there are just five notes in total, and they go like this: "Ru-hoo ru ru-hoo." Try counting the sounds next time you hear a wood pigeon in your garden.

There is a song in your mouth. Did you know that? It is a song of bold testimony:

He lifted me out of the slimy pit,
out of the mud and mire;
he set my feet on a rock
and gave me a firm place to stand.
He put a new song in my mouth,
a hymn of praise to our God.
Many will see and fear the LORD
and put their trust in him.

Psalm 40:2-3

(1) Many will see; (2) many will fear; and (3) many will trust in the Lord!

Oh sing to the LORD a new song;
  sing to the LORD, all the earth.
Sing to the LORD, bless his name;
  tell of his salvation from day to day.

Psalm 96:1-2 (ESV)

Every day is an opportunity to sing His praises. We don't have to wait for Sunday or a corporate gathering to sing them. We can utter with our mouths the overflow of our hearts wherever we are. We should not be silent.

You turned my wailing into dancing;
  you removed my sackcloth and clothed me with joy,
that my heart may sing your praises and not be silent.
  LORD my God, I will praise you forever.

Psalm 30:11-12 (NIVUK)

Every day [with its new reasons] will I bless You [affectionately and gratefully praise You]; yes, I will praise Your name forever and ever.

Psalm 145:2 (AMP)

As the wood pigeon is distinctive by its unique sound, may we be known as belonging to the Lord by the words we sing and speak each day. Resound His praises, reiterate His goodness and pray that "many" will see and "many" will fear and "many" will trust in the Lord.

30

The Sky is Red

He replied, "When evening comes, you say, 'It will be fair weather, for the sky is red,' and in the morning, 'Today it will be stormy, for the sky is red and overcast.' You know how to interpret the appearance of the sky, but you cannot interpret the signs of the times."

Matthew 16:2-3 (NIVUK)

The digital revolution has transformed how we access weather forecasts. Smartphone apps offer highly localised predictions and can even state what might happen in a fortnight's time. Having weather information right at our fingertips when we're trying to plan our days or decide what to wear is comfortable and reassuring. Before the digital era our ancestors lived close to the land and by observing the natural world they learned to predict what the seasons would bring. Clouds, birds, animals and plants all provided clues. An old weather-predicting adage rhythmically states, 'Red sky at night, shepherds' delight. Red sky in morning, shepherds' warning.' We see similar words from Jesus in today's passage.

The sky provides us with clues, as do flora. When the air gets humid in the hours before rain, many wild flowers protectively close their petals, such as daisies. If the white petals are closed and you cannot see the yellow middle disc, it is not advisable to hang out your washing. The presence of the contrails of aeroplanes are an early sign of bad weather too. If these don't dissolve, it indicates that humidity is on its way and the sky will soon cloud over. As regards temperature, bees only leave the hive at temperatures above 12°C. Also, you'll never hear the chirping (technically called stridulating) of grasshoppers and crickets below 12°C. Check out an old farmer's almanac for more!

Let's go back to Jesus' point in Matthew 16:

You find it easy enough to forecast the weather – why can't you read the signs of the times?

Matthew 16:3 (MSG)

The Pharisees didn't read the clear signs of the first coming of Jesus, and many people are missing the clear signs which point to the second coming of Christ. The Gospels of Matthew, Mark and Luke each contain an account of Christ teaching His disciples what to watch for before He returns. Yet it is all too easy to get caught up in the details of life, weighed down by the effects of sin, and distracted by the cares of the world. As someone put it, "We think more about the stock market than the second coming." The prophecies in the Bible are being fulfilled in front our eyes; we need to be prepared and have oil in our vessel for His imminent return.

Paul says that Christians are those "who have longed for his appearing"[56]. Another translation uses the colourful terminology, "for all who eagerly look forward to His glorious return"[57]. Is there an excitement within you that His return is imminent? Do you truly love the thought of Christ's appearing? Do your thoughts, your words, your actions indicate that you are truly looking for, longing for and loving His appearing? Paul tells Titus, and us, we are to…

…renounce irreligion and worldly passions, and to live sober, upright, and godly lives in this world, awaiting our blessed hope, the appearing of the glory of our great God and Saviour Jesus Christ, who gave Himself for us to redeem us from all iniquity and to purify for Himself a people of his own who are zealous for good deeds.

Titus 2:12-14 (RSV)

He says in Philippians:

But our citizenship is in heaven. And we eagerly await a Saviour from there, the Lord Jesus Christ.

Philippians 3:20 (NIVUK)

---

[56] 2 Timothy 4:8 (NIVUK)
[57] 2 Timothy 4:8 (NLT)

May eager expectation encourage us to be vigilant and diligent, fuelling us to be faithful in service and to live our lives circumspectly, redeeming the time.

31

Pause to Think – You'll Have Cause to Thank

What shall I render to the LORD for all his benefits to me?

Psalm 116:12 (ESVUK)

*E*merson said that if the stars came out only once a year, everybody would stay up all night to behold them. We have seen the stars so often that we don't bother to cast them a glance anymore. We have grown accustomed to our blessings. In Exodus 16 we can read of how God miraculously provided manna for the people to eat.

When the Israelites saw it, they said to each other, "What is it?" For they did not know what it was. Moses said to them, "It is the bread the LORD has given you to eat."

Exodus 16:15 (NIV)

The Hebrew word translated "manna" literally means 'What is it?' It was a brand-new way in which God was working in their lives. These Israelites in the wilderness, however, got accustomed to their blessings and God had to chasten them. It's easy to lose perspective. We all face challenges and difficulties in life. If we are not on guard, they can divert our attention from all the Lord has done for us.

Now the people complained about their hardships in the hearing of the Lord. … The rabble with them began to crave other food, and again the Israelites started wailing and said, "If only we had meat to eat! We remember the fish we ate in Egypt at no cost – also the cucumbers, melons, leeks, onions and garlic. But now we have lost our appetite; we never see anything but this manna!"

Numbers 11:1,4-6 (NIVUK)

When we direct our focus on the *things we don't have*, it causes us to minimise or forget all the blessings we do have. God had fed the nation

with heavenly manna each morning, and yet the people were getting tired
of it.

> *"But now our whole being is dried up," they said, "there is*
> *nothing at all except this manna before our eyes!"*
>
> *Numbers 11:6 (NKJV)*

Nothing but manna! They were experiencing a miracle of God's
provision every morning, yet they were no longer excited about it.
Nothing but manna! One of the evidences that we have grown
accustomed to our blessings is this spirit of criticism and complaining.
The spirit of entitlement and ingratitude pervades our culture and can all
too easily permeate our persona. Instead of thanking God for what we
have, we complain about it and tell Him we wish we had something else.
Would the people who live nearest to you characterise you as a
complaining person or a thankful person? Complaining is unbecoming
of a true Christian and yet we are proficient at it. The cure is found in
these verses, which Paul spoke to Timothy:

> *If we have food and covering, with these we shall be content.*
>
> *1 Timothy 6:8 (NASB)*

Elsewhere, we read that he learnt to be content in any circumstance,[58]
and it was the constant presence of Christ which made his contentment
possible.[59] Remind yourself today of these words:

> *Blessed be the Lord, who daily bears us up; God is our*
> *salvation. Selah.*
>
> *Psalm 68:19 (ESVUK)*

> *What shall I render to the LORD for all his benefits to me?*
>
> *Psalm 116:12 (ESVUK)*

> *Because of the LORD's great love we are not consumed, for his*
> *compassions never fail.*
>
> *Lamentations 3:22 (NIV)*

---

[58] See Philippians 4:11
[59] See Hebrews 13:5

Thankfulness is a core part of our lives as followers of Jesus. We are not only to be thankful; we are to be "abounding in thanksgiving"[60]. We have so much to be grateful for in this life each and every day.

---

[60] Colossians 2:7 (ESVUK)

November

November

1

Flower Clock

And that, knowing the time, that now it is high time to awake out of sleep: for now is our salvation nearer than when we believed. The night is far spent, the day is at hand: let us therefore cast off the works of darkness, and let us put on the armour of light.

Romans 13:11-12 (KJV)

*I*n 1751 Carl Linnaeus, in a treatise called *Philosophia Botanica*, proposed a concept known as the Horologium Florae (lit. 'a flower clock'). It was a garden plan to tell the time structured around the hypothesis that different plants open their flowers at different points in the day. It was a round flower bed split into twelve segments. Each segment of the flower clock represented exactly one hour of the day and was filled with plants in such a way that flowers opened or closed at a moment corresponding precisely to the time of day. Who needs a watch when the flowers know the time? Apparently, poppies alert us that it is 5am; bindweed at 6am; coltsfoot at 7am. From 8am marigolds spread out their golden petals, and daisies follow at 9am. You get the picture. After doing the longest shift, poppies shut up shop at around 6pm. Some species have adopted a late-opening strategy, such as evening primrose. I'm not sure how accurately a flower clock tells the time or if these flowers awake regularly each day despite weather conditions.

How accurately do we know the time and are we awake? The alarm has sounded. Like a trumpet call, Paul's words stir us to spiritual vigilance and zealous service. He says, it's not only time, it is *high time*. What does "high" time mean? We use it today in sentences such as, "It's high time I returned that library book," or, "It's high time you children were in bed." The precise meaning of this term depends on the tone of voice and the context. Paul used it in such a way as to indicate urgency. The Roman Christians had fallen into a kind of somnambulistic state. They were walking around asleep, asleep to their responsibilities and opportunities, asleep to the need and the challenge of the hour. Their society was being swamped by a sea of religious pluralism, yet they remained oblivious and unconcerned. Do we need to hear Paul's awakening words today? It is high time to awake out of sleep. We are to keep our lamps burning, our loins girded in a state of watchfulness. We are living in the time in which the Kingdom of heaven is likened by the Lord Jesus to "ten virgins who took their lamps and went out to meet the bridegroom"[61], and of these He said:

> *"While the bridegroom tarried they all slumbered and slept. And at midnight there was a cry made, Behold the bridegroom comes; go ye out to meet him. Then all those virgins arose and trimmed their lamps."*
>
> *Matthew 25:5-7 (KJV)*

For some the soporific influences of the world prevailed against them and they lapsed into that condition of lethargy. Others were ready with oil in their lamps.

Why do we need to wake up? Paul says:

> *The hour has come for you to wake up from your slumber, because our salvation is nearer now than when we first believed. The night is nearly over; the day is almost here.*
>
> *Romans 13:11-12 (NIV)*

We can't reach over and hit the 'snooze' button; it's time to wake up. May the Holy Spirit impress on our hearts the urgency of the hour.

---

[61] Matthew 25:1

2

From Every Language

After this I looked, and there before me was a great multitude that no one could count, from every nation, tribe, people and language, standing before the throne and before the Lamb. They were wearing white robes and were holding palm branches in their hands.

Revelation 7:9

English speakers may not be famous for being *au fait* with foreign languages, but all of us use words taken from other languages every day. There are so many common English words adopted from other languages, but they are so embedded into our everyday speech that we don't even realise that they weren't English originally. Some are adopted from:

- *France* – ballet, cafe, entrepreneur, genre, renaissance, rendezvous, cul-de-sac, garage;
- *German* – delicatessen, kindergarten, waltz, rucksack, glitch, hamster;
- *Spanish* – macho, patio, siesta, plaza, tornado;
- *Japanese* – karaoke, karate, origami, tsunami;
- *Arabic* – alcohol, algebra, average, artichoke, safari, sofa, zero, orange, mattress;
- *Irish* – boycott, hooligan, brogues, galore;
- *Hindi* – jungle, dinghy, pyjama, chutney, bangles, shampoo, bungalow;
- *Italian* – piano, alto, soprano, tempo, motto, studio, umbrella, balcony, regatta.

Our verse today reminds us that in front of the throne and before the Lamb there will be a vast crowd from every nation and tribe and people and language. From every language people will worship God.

And they sang a new song, saying, "Worthy are you to take the scroll and to open its seals, for you were slain, and by your blood you ransomed people for God from every tribe and language and people and nation, and you have made them a kingdom and priests to our God, and they shall reign on the earth."

Revelation 5:9-10

Today we face a task unfinished in terms of global outreach and fulfilling the Great Commission to go and make disciples of all nations.[62] So much progress has been made in recent years thanks to modern technology and pioneering missionary work. It is a time of unprecedented opportunity to share the glorious gospel of our Lord Jesus Christ. Never have the spiritual fields been so ripe for harvest. Mark 16:15 reminds us:

"Go into all the world and preach the gospel to all creation."

Mark 16:15

Your specific assignment is to reach every person in every group where you have influence. You are a channel of the love of God which has been poured into your heart. You are a conduit of His anointing which destroys yokes, removes burdens and sets the captives free. You are a carrier of His presence into the highways and byways of every strata of society within your reach.[63]

It is not a time to recede but a time to re-seed as we sow the Word of God into the nations. We are commissioned by the Lord;[64] we are compelled by His love.[65] What a difference it would make if we all obediently did our part to spread the gospel to every nation, tribe, people and language.

---

[62] See Matthew 28:18-20
[63] See Luke 14:23
[64] See Matthew 28:19-20
[65] See 2 Corinthians 5:14

3

A Soft Answer

A soft answer turns away wrath, but grievous words stir up anger.

Proverbs 15:1 (AMPC)

When I moved to live in County Kildare, I was greeted at the petrol pumps with the words, "It's a grand soft day." I politely agreed with the chap, not quite sure as to what I was assenting. Now I know that a soft day is a description of the weather and is probably very unique to the Emerald Isle. An inability to converse fluently and at length about the forecast is a true social impediment in Ireland, but I soon amassed a glossary of useful terms, including "a soft day". How can I describe it to you? A soft day is not the kind of day which includes a couple of hours of proper rain. It's not really rain, more a pervasive mist or slight drizzle that seems to get under your clothes and wet them from the inside out.

In Proverbs I stumbled across the word "soft" in a more positive light. What does Solomon mean by "a soft answer"? The Hebrew word he used, translated in our text as "soft", is *rak* and means 'soft, tender, gentle'. Proverbs has a lot to say about our words. In fact, we are taught that our words are powerful.

Death and life are in the power of the tongue...

Proverbs 18:21 (KJV)

Here in our verse we are shown that it is not only important to say the right words, but to say them in the right way. It refers to the intonation, volume and pitch of our voices. To give a soft answer, you must pause, pray and ponder how Christ Himself would respond.

This verse is one of the most beneficial and beautiful counsels in the Bible. When someone criticises you, simply give a soft answer. Don't respond in kind; respond in kindness. Speak with a gentle and gracious spirit and with genuine concern and compassion. A soft or gentle answer is much more effective than harsh words. When we produce the fruit of the Spirit instead of the fruit of the flesh, it displays the power of God in our lives. Instead of aggravating and escalating the problem, the verse says that a soft answer turns away wrath or deflects anger. On the other hand, grievous words stir up anger. The word "stir" is an interesting one. It means 'to cause something to take off, to ascend or to go to another level'. We are very wise when we choose not to escalate an argument with the way we speak our words. When we choose to answer softly, we will find God diffusing the volatile situation. May it be 'a soft day', especially as regards our words.

4

The Entrance of Esther

Now it came about on the third day that Esther put on her royal robes and stood in the inner court of the king's palace in front of the king's rooms, and the king was sitting on his royal throne in the throne room, opposite the entrance to the palace. When the king saw Esther the queen standing in the court, she obtained favour in his sight; and the king extended to Esther the golden sceptre which was in his hand. So Esther came near and touched the top of the sceptre. Then the king said to her, "What is troubling you, Queen Esther? And what is your request? Even to half of the kingdom it shall be given to you."

Esther 5:1-3 (NASB)

You know the story of Esther's courageous decision to approach King Ahasuerus to stop the wicked plans of Haman to destroy all the Jews. In Esther chapter five the Lord gives us a clear picture of the power of prayer – a specific type of prayer called intercession. We are given a visual resource of what it looks like when an intercessor approaches the throne of God's grace. Notice that Esther came humbly before the king in her royal apparel, clothed only in what he had provided for her. God has given us royal garments too, as Isaiah tells us:

I delight greatly in the Lord; my soul rejoices in my God. For he has clothed me with garments of salvation and arrayed me in a robe of righteousness.

Isaiah 61:10 (NIVUK)

Hebrews 10:19-22 tells us:

Therefore, brothers and sisters, since we have confidence to enter the Most Holy Place by the blood of Jesus, by a new and living way opened for us through the curtain, that is, his body, and since we have a great priest over the house of God, let us draw near to God with a sincere heart in full assurance of faith, having our hearts sprinkled to cleanse us from a guilty conscience and having our bodies washed with pure water.

Hebrews 10:19-22 (NIVUK)

Esther 5:2 shows how the king's sceptre was extended in grace. Isn't it wonderful how we can "approach the throne of God's grace with confidence"[66] "by the blood of Jesus"[67] in full assurance that our sins are forgiven?

We must never approach God on the basis of what we deserve, but rather on the basis of His mercy, which we can never deserve. Our confidence is not in our own abilities or our own righteousness – but in God's undeserved kindness, compassion and extravagant generosity.

It was said of Esther:

"And who knows but that you have come to royal position for such a time as this?"

Esther 4:14 (NIV)

We too are here for such as time as this. We are living in perilous times and we are born for this precise moment in history. We can impact nations and generations through our prayers of intercession by standing in the authority we have through Christ. Think about it: "Who knows but you have come to this place for such a time as this!" Our prayers matter. Our voice matters. May we be ever faithful to pray for all those in authority, for those who need someone to speak up on their behalf, for those who are being downtrodden or persecuted.

The king said to Esther, "What is *troubling* you, Queen Esther? And what is your request?"[68] What would you ask for? Are you burdened by the plight of others? What is on your heart most often when you approach the King? An intercessor does not pray solely for his or her own benefit. Rather, an intercessor recognises and is gripped by the peril of other people. Esther faced what seemed an impossible task, but she faithfully presented her huge request to the king and it was granted. We need to pray God-sized prayers on behalf of others, knowing "all things are possible with God".

---

[66] Hebrews 4:16 (NIV)
[67] Hebrews 10:19 (NIV)
[68] Emphasis added

5

Don't Be a Diotrephes

I wrote to the church, but Diotrephes, who loves to be first, will not welcome us. So when I come, I will call attention to what he is doing, spreading malicious nonsense about us. Not satisfied with that, he even refuses to welcome other believers. He also stops those who want to do so and puts them out of the church.

3 John 9-10 (NIVUK)

We probably all remember the one well-known spelling rule in English: 'i before e except after c'. We also know that there are all kinds of exceptions to this rule. On a teacher's mug I saw the words, "i before e except when your foreign neighbour Keith receives eight counterfeit beige sleighs from feisty caffeinated weightlifters – weird." The problem lies with the issue of where to put the 'i'. Does it come first or follow after?

A similar problem arose in the early church concerning someone called Diotrephes. Almost nothing is known about him except for what is tucked away neatly into verses 9-10 of third John. We are told, he loved to be first. He had an 'i first' mentality in contrast to what Jesus taught:

"Anyone who wants to be first must be the very last, and the servant of all."

Mark 9:35 (NIVUK)

Being self-asserting meant that Diotrephes was ungracious toward those who didn't agree with him. In fact, he maliciously gossiped about any whom he saw as a threat to his monopoly of power. He unjustly accused John, the beloved disciple of the Lord, and excommunicated loyal believers because they failed to side with him in his rejection of John's authority.

Paul said to the Philippians:

Do nothing out of selfish ambition or vain conceit. Rather, in humility value others above yourselves, not looking to your own interests but each of you to the interests of the others.

Philippians 2:3 (NIV)

Or, as another translation states:

Don't push your way to the front; don't sweet-talk your way to the top. Put yourself aside, and help others get ahead. Don't be obsessed with getting your own advantage. Forget yourselves long enough to lend a helping hand.

Philippians 2:3 (MSG)

A Diotrephes will be more concerned about building up and protecting his own reputation rather than looking out for the interests of others. He is a prime example of pride at work. Pride is a preoccupation with self. It is thus very fitting that the middle letter in the word 'pride' is 'i'. Likewise the middle letter in 'sin' is 'i'. We live in the 'me generation' where the proud spirit of Diotrephes reigns supreme. The challenge is clear. Could you and I be an unwittingly modern-day Diotrephes? Do we love attention at the expense of others? Do we insist on having our own way? Do we question the authority of Scripture and the apostles' teaching? Do we speak disparagingly about the church? Do we deem others unworthy of fellowship?

Search me, O God, and know my heart...

Psalm 139:23 (NKJV)

6

Our Walk with God

And Enoch walked with God; and he was not, for God took him.

Genesis 5:24 (NKJV)

The biography of Enoch is brief, only nine verses in all: five verses in Genesis, two in Hebrews and two in Jude. Enoch sojourned on earth during a strategic time in human history, prior to the Flood recorded in Genesis 6. It was recorded there that...

The LORD saw that the wickedness of man was great in the earth, and that every imagination and intention of all human thinking was only evil continually.

Genesis 6:5 (AMP)

However, in start contrast, it is refreshing to read of someone who was "commended as having pleased God"[69].

When Genesis 5 tells us that Enoch walked with God, this isn't just poetic rhetoric; this is practical reality. It is the powerful, pulsating principle which permeates his entire life. The minor prophet Amos threw out the challenge to each one of us:

Can two walk together, unless they are agreed?

Amos 3:3 (NKJV)

The Hebrew word for "together" speaks of union and rhythm and reminds me of synchronised divers and swimmers at the Olympic Games. Enoch's walk was choreographed and concurrent with the very heartbeat of God. This privilege was not for Enoch alone. The good news is that we too can walk daily with Him.

Paul told us:

---

[69] Hebrews 11:5 (ESV)

151

> *Therefore, as you received Christ Jesus the Lord, so walk in him, rooted and built up in him and established in the faith, just as you were taught.*
>
> *Colossians 2:6-7 (ESV)*

When we walk with the Lord, we are rewarded with light, direction, discernment, revelation. He speaks to us distinctly amid the details of our day saying, "This is the way, walk in it."[70] We become sensitive to the overtures of His Spirit and desire to honour Him in all ways. He is our Companion, our Counsellor, our Confidante in the path of life. As we walk with Him, we learn to have His outlook and see life from His perspective. The desires of His heart become the desires of our hearts. For Enoch, God was not some distant cosmic cause; He was and is intimately relational.

In the account of his life in Hebrews we are told that Enoch not only walked with God, he was well pleasing to God.

> *He was commended as having pleased God. And without faith it is impossible to please Him, for whoever would draw near to God must believe that He exists and that He rewards those who seek Him.*
>
> *Hebrews 11:5-6 (ESVUK)*

The Greek root word for "please" means 'fully united, wholly agreeable, in total oneness'. What's interesting is that this is exactly what the Lord said about His Son, Jesus:

> *"This is My beloved Son, in whom I am well pleased."*
>
> *Matthew 3:17 (NKJV)*

It is the will of God that we learn to walk in a manner pleasing to the Lord...

> *...that you may walk worthy of the Lord, fully pleasing Him, being fruitful in every good work and increasing in the knowledge of God...*
>
> *Colossians 1:10 (NKJV)*

Reflect on how you can make it your aim to consistently and intimately walk with God today. What might this mean for you?

---

[70] Isaiah 30:21 (NKJV)

7

Far from Home

So He told them this parable, saying, "What man among you,
if he has a hundred sheep and has lost one of them, does not
leave the ninety-nine in the open pasture and go after the one
which is lost until he finds it? When he has found it, he lays it
on his shoulders, rejoicing. And when he comes home, he calls
together his friends and his neighbours, saying to them,
'Rejoice with me, for I have found my sheep which was lost!'"

Luke 15:3-6 (NASB)

As I was ironing, the lunchtime news was airing in the background and my ears perked up when I heard one of the headlines: *A "very lost" beluga whale has been sighted in the River Thames "far from home". Experts tell us it is "in grave danger".*

Immediately my eyes welled up with emotion. The news reporter informed the public that belugas are commonly found in coastal waters of the Arctic Ocean and so this particular whale was thousands of miles off course and far removed from its usual habitat. Animal and marine charities were working together to help the whale return to the sea and had a medical team on standby in case it became beached. I found myself extremely distressed by the story and even prayed for its welfare! It was after this that God impressed on me, "How concerned are you for the many 'very lost' people around you 'far from home' and 'in grave danger'? Do you feel any concern for the spiritually lost?"

Jesus declared His life's mission in Luke 19:10:

"Indeed, the Son of Man has come to seek and to save people
who are lost."

Luke 19:10 (GW)

Jesus was all about people, and the closer you get to Him, the more His passion for souls will consume you and become the overwhelming force in your life. Do you share that same passion as Jesus Christ? He told us the parable of the sheep which was lost, recorded in Luke 15. When I looked up the New Testament Greek word for "lost", I found that is the same word that is translated "perish" in John 3:16. It means 'to be lost, ruined or destroyed'. The sheep was heading for destruction. The shepherd knew this and was concerned about the condition of the sheep. This shepherd saw the value in just one sheep, and he went after it. He knew that it was "very lost" and "far from home" and "in grave danger".

Our work of reaching the lost is not finished. As the hymn rightly states:

> *Facing a task unfinished,*
>   *that drives us to our knees.*
> *A need that, undiminished,*
>   *rebukes our slothful ease.*
> *We, who rejoice to know Thee,*
>   *renew before Thy throne,*
> *the solemn pledge we owe Thee*
>   *to go and make Thee known.*[71]

Think about the crowds you see in shopping malls and along busy streets who live "without hope and without God in the world"[72]. Think about your family and friends. Scripture tells us that when Jesus saw the crowds...

> *...he had compassion on them, because they were harassed and helpless, like sheep without a shepherd.*
>
> Matthew 9:36 (NIVUK)

We need to ask God to move our hearts with the same compassion that moves His heart. Our task is immense and it is urgent.

I checked the news again later but there was still no update on the situation of the beluga whale. I cannot assure you of a happy ending, but I do know this:

> *For God so loved the world that he gave his one and only Son, that whoever believes in him shall not perish but have eternal life. For God did not send his Son into the world to condemn the world, but to save the world through him. Whoever*

---

[71] *Facing a Task Unfinished;* Frank Houghton (1930)
[72] Ephesians 2:12 (HCSB)

believes in him is not condemned, but whoever does not believe stands condemned already because they have not believed in the name of God's one and only Son.

John 3:16-18 (NIVUK)

8

Hooping

"Martha, Martha, you are worried and bothered about so many things; but only one thing is necessary, for Mary has chosen the good part, which shall not be taken away from her."

Luke 10:41-42 (NASB)

I never quite mastered the art of hula hooping. Do you remember those plastic hula hoops with added bits of glitter and noisemakers for added effect? Children still love them and adults have begun using stronger, larger, heavier hoops for fitness and fun. Hula hoops are most commonly twirled, known as 'hooping', around the waist, but other parts of the body, including arms, legs and neck, are also used. The longest recorded duration for a single hula hoop to be hooped is 74 hours and 54 minutes, a record set in Ohio, United States by Aaron Hibbs in late 2009. The record for the most hoops twirled simultaneously is 160, set by Marawa the Amazing on April 7th 2014. In 2000, Roman Schedler spun a 53-pound tractor tyre for 71 seconds at the 5th Saxon Record Festival in Bregenz, Austria.

The key to successful hooping is to keep moving. Don't stop. It's all about the action. In Luke 10 we read the familiar story in which Martha is all action too; she's scurrying around the kitchen like a whirlwind, checking the roast lamb, setting the table and icing the cake. Jesus is visiting and she is busy preparing dinner for her honoured guest. Mary, her co-host, should be helping but instead she sits at the feet of Jesus listening to Him, and He teaches. She prioritises the Lord's presence. Exasperated, Martha finally appeals to Jesus:

"Lord, do you not care that my sister has left me to serve alone? Tell her then to help me."

Luke 10:40 (ESV)

Jesus responds to her:

"Martha, Martha, you are worried and bothered about so many things; but only one thing is necessary, for Mary has chosen the good part, which shall not be taken away from her."

Luke 10:41-42 (NASB)

Jesus does not negate Martha's serving but He does berate her for being worried and bothered about it. Although her intentions are good, they ultimately take her attention off of the one thing that matters most, which is her relationship with Jesus.

What is it that Jesus wants us to learn from this experience? What application can we draw from Jesus' words that will have meaning to us amidst the stresses and struggles of modern society? "Martha, Martha..." Put your name there, on the lips of Jesus. Maybe He's speaking to you and reminding you, "You are worried and bothered by so many things." When you feel this way, stop and take a deep breath. Ask yourself if you've done the one thing that is really necessary today. Have you sat at Jesus' feet?

When we concentrate on Jesus first, we discover that we are never truly alone or without help.[73] We experience that His grace is sufficient for all that we face.[74] We find inner peace and strength to face whatever comes our way.[75] We discover that when we listen to His words and heed them, He makes our way prosperous and gives us good success.[76] Our serving needs to flow from a place of fellowship, of intimacy, of love for Jesus. The correct priority for our lives is shown in Mark 3:14:

...He appointed twelve ... that they might be with him and that he might send them out to preach...

Mark 3:14 (NKJV)

We spend time in fellowship with Jesus and then go to work. It's so easy to let our worries and the length of our to-do lists draw us away from the only thing that is necessary: a relationship with Jesus. How freeing it is to realise that it's "necessary" to take time to sit still in His presence and let Him feed our souls.

---

[73] See Hebrews 13:5
[74] See 2 Corinthians 9:8
[75] See John 14:27
[76] See Joshua 1:8-9

9

Save Our Socks

Whoever looks intently into the perfect law ... and continues in it – not forgetting what they have heard, but doing it – they will be blessed in what they do.

James 1:25 (NIV)

Scientists are trying to solve one of life's mysteries – why so many socks go missing in the wash. You know the phenomenon: you do your laundry, which contains at least several pairs of socks. But when you start to fold your clothes after taking them out of the dryer, lo and behold, two socks are missing. Over the course of time you are left with a pile of lonely items that have lost their other half. According to the findings of a serious scientific study conducted in the UK, the average person loses:

- 1.3 socks each month, which equates to;
- more than 15 socks a year, which equates to;
- 1,264 lost socks over a lifetime, which costs the individual;
- £2,528.

In all, these laundry losses mean around eighty-four million socks go missing every month in the UK. While many are willing to accept that there is a Bermuda Triangle for socks, others are trying to come up with more interesting and realistic theories. One such is that the sock has not actually disappeared. Instead, the sock is simply no longer observable. We don't look closely enough in our search. Instead of peering behind radiators or under beds, we accept the remaining sock as a singular entity, experience a brief grieving process and go on with our lives. Their small size and susceptibility to static cling makes them ideal candidates to wind up in sweaters, jackets and fitted sheets. Sometimes they are simply left in the drum of the machine and we fail to notice because we do not bother to stoop down and peer in.

James, in chapter one, encourages us to bend over and peer into God's Word, the Bible. He tells us in verse 25 to "look intently" into it and the Greek word he uses is *parakupto* which means 'to stoop or bend in order to look into'. Prior to this verse, James told us how we can easily deceive ourselves:

> But don't just listen to God's word. You must do what it says. Otherwise, you are only fooling yourselves. For if you listen to the word and don't obey, it is like glancing at your face in a mirror. You see yourself, walk away, and forget what you look like.
>
> *James 1:22-24 (NLT)*

Such an action sounds absurd to us. After all, the reason you look in a mirror is to see yourself and note what might need adjustment. Otherwise, why would you bother looking?

Surely, we look in the mirror and adjust our lives accordingly. Is my hair just right? Do I have a grain of pepper in my teeth?

Christians should look intently into the perfect law, the law that gives freedom. When we routinely do that and obey what we see there, we will be blessed in what we do. Don't just give it a casual glance each day. We want to look fully and deeply into the Word of God to see what it says for our lives. It brings us freedom. Jesus said in John chapter eight:

> If you continue in my word, you really are my disciples. You will know the truth, and the truth will set you free.
>
> *John 8:31-32 (HCSB)*

Some people view Bible reading and study as a burden similar to emptying the rubbish bin, or flossing, or cleaning the bathtub. However, the Word of God is like a vault, full of wisdom and riches waiting to be mined. Look intently and discover His precious and exceedingly great promises for you.

10

Twinkle, Twinkle

Then God said, "Let there be lights in the expanse of the heavens to separate the day from the night, and let them be for signs and for seasons and for days and years; and let them be for lights in the expanse of the heavens to give light on the earth"; and it was so. God made the two great lights, the greater light to govern the day, and the lesser light to govern the night; He made the stars also.

Genesis 1:14-16 (NASB)

Twinkle, twinkle, little star
How I wonder what you are
Up above the world so high
Like a diamond in the sky.

*I*n one of my clearest childhood memories I am walking with my father and looking into the inky canopy of the night sky searching for what he called the Big Dipper (The Plough). It was and still is stunningly beautiful, even to the unaided eye. Some of you may have had the experience of camping out under the surreal blanket of the stars, unmasked by artificial light.

It is amazing to look up at the sparkling brilliance of the Milky Way knowing that the magnitude and immensity of the sky exceeds our finite gaze and limited knowledge. It all reflects the overwhelming majesty, power and awesomeness of our Creator, the great I AM, who is above all and before all and beyond all.

Genesis begins with the account of how God created the heavens and the earth. But in just five simple words, almost like an afterthought, it tells us, "...he made the stars also."[77] The economy of words here is so staggering. It is astonishing that the creation of the entire universe beyond earth is described so casually by such a simple statement.

---

[77] Genesis 1:16 (KJV)

The psalmist eloquently tells us:

The heavens declare the glory of God;
the skies proclaim the work of his hands.

Psalm 19:1 (NIVUK)

This sweeping declaration reveals the influence and impact of creation. It points us to God and proclaims His Glory. In Psalm 8:3-4, the psalmist says:

When I consider Your heavens, the work of Your fingers,
the moon and the stars, which You have ordained;
what is man that You take thought of him,
and the son of man that You care for him?

Psalm 8:3-4 (ESV)

No wonder he opened and closed the same psalm with the remark:

O LORD, our Lord, how majestic is Your name in all the earth.

Psalm 8:9 (ESV)

God speaks to us through the prophet Isaiah saying:

"So who will you compare me with?
Who is equal to me?" says the Holy One.
Look up toward the sky.
Who created everything you see?
The LORD causes the stars to come out at night one by one.
He calls out each one of them by name.
His power and strength are great.
So none of the stars is missing.

Isaiah 40:25-26 (NIRV)

God asks in Job:

"Can you bind the cluster of the Pleiades,
Or loose the belt of Orion?
Can you bring out Mazzaroth in its season?
Or can you guide the Great Bear with its cubs?"

Job 38:31-32 (NKJV)

May we take time to look up, observe His handiwork and recognise His majesty and splendour on display.

11

The Dirtiest Things You Touch Every Day

Come near to God and he will come near to you. Wash your hands, you sinners, and purify your hearts, you double-minded.

James 4:8 (NIVUK)

*S*ome of the things you touch are absolutely teeming with bacteria. The top culprits are dishcloths, door handles and light switches, not to mention your toothbrush. That brush you've been running over your pearly whites probably has more germs than your dog's entire mouth. Our toothbrushes tend to be close to our toilets – and if you flush with the toilet lid up, everything within a five to six foot radius is getting sprayed with aerosolised faecal matter. Other contenders are keys and remote controls. You should see what scientists have detected on hotel room remotes: an average of 67.6 colony-forming units of bacteria per cubic centimetre. The list of dirtiest items continues: mobile phones, grocery trolleys, computer keyboards, money, restaurant menus. Bacteria and viruses can survive up to eighteen hours on an object, and adults touch up to thirty different objects in a minute, thus allowing bacteria and germs to crawl onto the skin. So hand sanitiser at the ready, please!

Keeping our hands clean is one of the best ways to prevent the spread of infection and illness. "Wash your hands" is also the command of James in today's verse. He is calling his readers to a radical repentance. They had become stained with worldliness.

Come close to God and He will come close to you. [Recognise that you are] sinners, get your soiled hands clean; [realise that you have been disloyal] wavering individuals with divided interests, and purify your hearts [of your spiritual adultery].

James 4:8 (AMPC)

James had already exhorted his readers to keep themselves "unspotted and uncontaminated from the world"[78]. Now he says that they have settled for what they thought was a happy compromise between sold-out commitment to God and a worldly lifestyle. He therefore makes the choice clear: if we are going to draw near to God, we need to deal decisively with worldliness. There must be genuine sorrow for all unfaithfulness, as James goes on to say in the next verse.

> *Be afflicted, and mourn, and weep...*
>
> *James 4:9 (KJV)*

The first verb refers to the inward feeling of wretchedness, the other two to the outward expression of it. It's all about the true repentance.

The priests were commanded to cleanse their hands and their feet at the laver before drawing near to God in the Holy Place. Psalm 24 asks:

> *Who shall ascend the hill of the LORD?*
> *And who shall stand in his holy place?*
> *He who has clean hands and a pure heart,*
> *who does not lift up his soul to what is false,*
> *and does not swear deceitfully.*
>
> *Psalm 24:3-5 (ESVUK)*

The requirement for ascending to the place of God in worship is that our hands are clean and our hearts purified. May we take time today to draw near to God with "clean hands and a pure heart".

---

[78] James 1:27 (AMPC)

12

"Me First" Mentality

Now it happened as they journeyed on the road, that someone said to Him, "Lord, I will follow You wherever You go." And Jesus said to him, "Foxes have holes and birds of the air have nests, but the Son of Man has nowhere to lay His head." Then He said to another, "Follow Me." But he said, "Lord, let me first go and bury my father." ... And another also said, "Lord, I will follow You, but let me first go and bid them farewell who are at my house."

Luke 9:57-59,61 (NKJV)

There are a couple of phrases which you will never need to teach your toddler: "It's mine!" and "Me first!" We all come pre-wired to put ourselves in first place. Did you notice the words, "me first" in the verses above? In the Gospels – Matthew, Mark, Luke and John – Jesus' command to "follow me" appears repeatedly. As He went about His earthly ministry, people wanted to follow Him, but some desired to do so on their own terms rather than being fully committed to Him as Lord. He is saying, "Follow *me*." But they answer:

"Lord, let *me first* go and bury my father."

"Lord, I will follow you, but let *me first* go and bid them farewell..."

In this passage from Luke, people admire Jesus and are inspired by Him and say, "I will follow you." But they remind Him that they have their own concerns to deal with first. The "me first" mentality supposes all of life is engineered to somehow suit *me*. In a culture that focuses on "me first", it is important to understand that God does not function in the same way. In fact, Jesus states that we are to seek first the Kingdom of God, not our own wants, desires and feelings.[79] He also taught His disciples:

---

[79] See Matthew 6:33

"If anyone would come after me, let him deny himself and take up his cross daily and follow me."

Luke 9:23 (ESVUK)

It's a call to absolute surrender of self. He said "take up his cross daily"; He didn't say once in a while or when it's convenient. He said *daily*. In Jesus' day, a cross wasn't just a symbol of pain and suffering; it was mainly a symbol of death. What Jesus was telling them is that they needed to put to death their own plans and desires and then turn their lives over to Him and do His will every day.

Following Jesus is easy when life runs smoothly; our true commitment to Him is revealed during trials. Jesus assured us that trials will come to His followers[80] and so it is important that we count the cost. Challenge yourself: have you put to death your own plans and committed yourself to His will for your life? Is your following of Jesus conditional on things going smoothly? Contrast the total commitment of Jesus to doing his Father's will with the preconditions and qualifications which we can make in response to his call to discipleship. Discipleship is a radical call which requires our wholehearted response and there is no room for a "me first" mentality.

---

[80] See John 16:33

13

Food for Thought: Menu or Meal?

Jesus says, "You search the Scriptures because you think that in them you have eternal life; and it is they that bear witness about me, yet you refuse to come to me that you may have life."

John 5:39-40 (ESVUK)

*L*et me begin with a rather strange question: would you prefer the menu or the meal? The word 'menu', like much of the terminology of cuisine, is French in origin. It ultimately derives from the Latin word *minutus*, meaning 'something made small'. The original menus were written on a small chalkboard, in French a *carte;* so foods chosen from a menu today are described as *à la carte*, 'according to the board'. Apparently, rather than read menus from front to back, diners today tend to scan them quickly (spending an average of just 109 seconds, according to a Gallup poll). This means that a menu has a small amount of time to make a big impact. Most prefer short and concise choices rather than the complexity of a periodic table. People are more likely to order something with a description than without it. For example, 'caramelised' has mesmeric power. Adjectives like 'line-caught', 'farm-raised' or 'locally-sourced' are also magnets for customers.

The idea behind the menu is that you order the meal and enjoy it. The Bible tells us to "taste and see that the LORD is good"[81]. The Bible is the menu meant to lead us to experience God and His goodness in every facet of our lives. But Jesus criticised the Pharisees for reading and scrutinising the Scripture but missing its entire purpose: coming to Him. They studied the menu but did not order the meal. As Jack Deere has said in his book, *Surprised by the Voice of God:*

> *The Bible is the menu and Jesus Christ is the meal ... If our Bible study doesn't lead us to an experience of Jesus Christ*

---

[81] Psalm 34:8 (ESVUK)

then we are like the Pharisees who were holding the menu, reading the menu and studying the menu, but they were so far from the meal.[82]

Bible study is essential but some people make "searching the Scriptures" an end in itself. They are like people who study a menu with great precision and can tell you every detail about it: when it was first written, font size, layout etc. However, there is the danger that they end up just like the Pharisees who searched the Scriptures diligently but never came to Christ. They studied the menu regularly and religiously, but they never ordered, never tasted.

Jesus said, "...you refuse to come to me that you may have life." He was not saying that the Scriptures were unimportant or that the Jews were wrong in revering them. The point He was making is that they were missing the point. The point of the Scriptures is to lead us to the Person of Jesus and help us to know Him more and more. I love the way that Dr. Mark Strauss puts it:

Our passion should not be for scripture per se, but for the One who reveals himself in the scriptures.[83]

When Jesus had a Bible study with two Emmaus disciples after His crucifixion and resurrection, Luke records the event by telling us:

And beginning with Moses and with all the prophets, He explained to them the things concerning Himself in all the Scriptures.

Luke 24:27 (NASB)

Later that evening in Jerusalem, Jesus had another Bible study with most of the disciples and a few other believers who were gathered in a private room. Luke again tells us what He said:

Now He said to them, "These are My words which I spoke to you while I was still with you, that all things which are written about Me in the Law of Moses and the Prophets and the

---

[82] Jack Deere; *Surprised by the Voice of God;* revised edition; Zondervan Academic (1998); p175

[83] Mark Strauss; *How to Read the Bible in Changing Times;* Bakerbooks; p71

Psalms must be fulfilled." Then He opened their minds to understand the Scriptures.

Luke 24:44-45 (NASB)

Don't stop with reading the menu; but make sure you sample the meal.

14

Topiary Tips

...for it is God who is at work in you, both to will and to work for His good pleasure.

Philippians 2:13 (NASB)

Over the years I have visited a number of stately houses immersing myself in the history and heritage dotted all around Northern Ireland. The houses are architecturally ambitious and extravagant, but it is usually the acres of pristine manicured gardens, crunchy gravel paths and displays of traditional topiary which amaze me most. Topiary is the horticultural art of clipping and trimming the foliage of shrubs or trees into ornamental shapes. Peacocks, swans, orbs, spirals and pyramids are a few ideas in case you feel inspired to add definition to your garden! Don't forget that stylised or sculpted greenery is achieved best with malleable material (yew, box or rosemary are the classics). It also helps to visualise the final outcome before you start clipping.

As I thought of the art of topiary today, I imagined God shaping our lives in similar fashion. Waking up feeling purposeless each day is not part of His plan for us. Rather, the One who authored our lives desires that we each live a passionate, engaged, meaningful life. God sees our beginning and our ending all at once. He is the one who has planned all of our days and therefore He knows what's best for us – all the time. He is the One who can bring definition to our lives.

Don't let the world around you squeeze you into its own mould, but let God re-mould your minds from within, so that you may prove in practice that the plan of God for you is good, meets all his demands and moves towards the goal of true maturity.

Romans 12:2 (JBP)

He wants to mould and shape us but the question is, *am I malleable?* Are you? Do we have malleable hearts softened by exposure to God's Word? Do we yield to His way of doing things?

> *Neither yield ye your members as instruments of unrighteousness unto sin: but yield yourselves unto God, as those that are alive from the dead, and your members as instruments of righteousness unto God.*
>
> Romans 6:13 (KJV)

What does it mean to yield to God? The Amplified translation is informative here:

> *Do not go on offering members of your body to sin as instruments of wickedness. But offer yourselves to God [in a decisive act]...*
>
> Romans 6:13 (AMP)

God wants us to yield, or present, our bodies to Him. Having a yielded heart means that we trust Him. When I talk about trusting God, I'm talking about putting our faith completely in Him, giving Him control of our life, trusting Him with the results, trusting Him to deal with whatever comes our way. With the malleable material of our submissive hearts He can shape and stylise our lives according to His purpose. James encourages each one of us:

> *So let God work his will in you.*
>
> James 4:7 (MSG)

Are we ready? God holds the secateurs which can trim off the superfluous from our lives. Regarding all that is unnecessary and overgrowth, God says, "Let's get rid of this. Let's throw off all that hinders – throw aside every encumbrance (unnecessary weight)."[84] Allow Him to clip away those undesirable attitudes and rake away the rubble. Remember this: God is intentionally working on us today.

---

[84] See Hebrews 12:1

15

Don't Bite the Bait of Bitterness

Let all bitterness and wrath and anger and clamour and slander be put away from you, along with all malice. Be kind to one another, tender-hearted, forgiving each other, just as God in Christ also has forgiven you.

Ephesians 4:31-32 (ESVUK)

A boat hook, fenders, oars, maritime radio, echo sounder, compass, chart, binoculars, lifejacket and flares are some of the basic boating equipment. One of the oldest and most basic pieces of equipment found aboard any boat is the anchor. One of my least favourite exercises while boating was weighing anchor. Weighing anchor literally means raising the anchor of the vessel from the sea floor and hoisting it up. Pulling an anchor off the bottom hand-over-hand in the best of conditions is a lot of work. Add the pressure of currents and the work is compounded.

In today's verse, the Greek word Paul used for "be put away" is *airo* and it means 'to lift up something, such as an anchor of a ship to that the ship could set sail'. The same word appears in Acts where Paul was journeying by ship towards Rome:

When a gentle south wind began to blow, they saw their opportunity; so they weighed anchor and sailed along the shore of Crete.

Acts 27:13 (NIVUK)

The idea of the word in context of our verse today is that bitterness is pulling us down and we need to give it the *heave ho*. It's not a suggestion; it's a command. The book of Hebrews warns us about allowing bitterness to take root:

See to it that no one falls short of the grace of God and that no bitter root grows up to cause trouble and defile many.

Hebrews 12:15 (NIVUK)

Bitterness is always waiting for a place to take root in our lives. The word for "bitterness" is *pikros;* it literally means 'sharp, piercing' and it is self-destructive. It is a poison which can debilitate you physically, depress you emotionally and dominate you mentally. It also affects you spiritually. That's why Paul called for zero tolerance. "Let all bitterness … be put away from you." *All.*

Is there any bitterness in your heart against anyone? If you allow bitterness a place in your heart, it will eventually come out of your mouth in murmuring and complaining.

Bitterness always inflicts a deeper wound on the person who harbours it than the person against whom it is directed. I recall an incidence where a man who had car trouble on a lonely road asked a farmer to tow him to the nearest garage. On the way, his wife was protesting to her husband about the fee which the farmer was charging.

"It is scandalous," she said, "to charge us so much for towing this car only three miles."

To which her husband replied, "Never mind, dear. I'm having my revenge – I've got my brakes on."

Many a person has thought himself to be getting revenge, but all the time the major damage was being done to him. Bitterness is unbecoming to such as are born again, and grieving to the Spirit of God. The word is in contrast with the beautiful epithet, "…be kind to each other, tenderhearted, forgiving one another,"[85] in the following verse. Let us show the kind of love, kindness and forgiveness that Christ has given to us.

---

[85] Ephesians 4:32 (NLT)

16

Call Upon the Name of the Lord

But Ananias answered, "Lord, I have heard from many about this man, how much harm he did to Your saints at Jerusalem; and here he has authority from the chief priests to bind all who call on Your name."

Acts 9:13-14 (ESVUK)

Call upon the name of the Lord. Those words keep appearing every time I turn to God's Word. God has identified his people as those who call upon His name. The first mention of it occurs in Genesis:

Seth also had a son, and he named him Enosh. At that time, people began to call on the name of the LORD.

Genesis 4:26 (NIVUK)

Why did people begin to do this? The meaning of the name Enosh provides us with a clue. It means 'frail, mortal man'. From the time of Enosh, people realised both the emptiness and futility of life apart from God as well as their own fragility and mortality. They realised their desperate need of God. The history of calling on the Lord's name continued throughout the Bible with Abraham who "built an altar to the LORD and called upon the name of the LORD"[86]. You can check out Isaac[87], Moses[88], Jabez[89], Samson[90], Samuel[91], David[92], Jonah[93], Elijah[94]

---

[86] Genesis 12:8 (ESV)
[87] See Genesis 26:25
[88] See Deuteronomy 4:7
[89] See 1 Chronicles 4:10
[90] See Judges 16:28
[91] See 1 Samuel 12:18
[92] See 2 Samuel 22:4
[93] See Jonah 1:6
[94] See 1 Kings 18:24

and Jeremiah[95], to name a few examples. In Psalm 116 calling on the Lord is mentioned four times.[96] The literal translation of the Hebrew word *qara* means 'to cry out, or to implore aid'. Other nations may have had their horses and chariots, but God's people simply called upon His Name. Whenever they stopped calling upon Him, they were defeated and humiliated.

Calling on the name of the Lord was practised by the New Testament believers beginning on the day of Pentecost.[97] Saul of Tarsus received authority from the chief priests to bind all that called on the name of the Lord.[98] They called upon the name of Jesus, and that became a mark of recognition. Thus, Saul of Tarsus felt that it would be easy to identify the Christians in Damascus by the fact that they called on the Lord's name. How identifiable are we today? Are we calling upon the name of the Lord? As believers in Christ, we should call on the Lord daily[99] and for as long as we live[100].

In the Bible I found a verse which defined workers of iniquity or evildoers in the following way:

> *Have all the workers of iniquity no knowledge, who eat up*
> *my people as they eat bread and who do not call on the Lord?*
>
> *Psalm 14:4 (AMPC)*

They refuse to call upon the name of the Lord. They will not humble themselves to recognise His omnipotence by calling on His name with all their hearts. Humanity's condition is similar today as it was in the time of Enosh. We are still weak, frail and mortal, and life is often full of turmoil and trouble. We need the eternal God and His plenteous mercy. However low we feel, He is only a prayer away.

> *Seek ye the Lord while he may be found, call ye upon him*
> *while he is near: Let the wicked forsake his way, and the*
> *unrighteous man his thoughts: and let him return unto the*

---

[95] See Lamentations 3:55
[96] verses 2,4,13,17
[97] See Acts 2:21
[98] See Acts 9:14
[99] See Psalm 88:9
[100] See Psalm 116:2

Lord, and he will have mercy upon him; and to our God, for he will abundantly pardon.

Isaiah 55:6-7 (KJV)

I called upon Your name, O Lord, out of the lowest pit. You have heard my voice.

Lamentations 3:55 (AMP)

We may call on His name at any time and in any place.

17

A Holy Discontent

After they prayed, the place where they were meeting was shaken. And they were all filled with the Holy Spirit and spoke the word of God boldly.

Acts 4:31 (NIV)

*L*eonard Ravenhill was a man with a real heart for revival. He said, "As long as we are content to live without revival, we will." We can go on day after day, week after week, year after year, stating our desire for revival but being content to live without it. Or we can ask God for a holy discontent for anything less than His reviving work in our hearts and through our lives. A holy discontent primes our lives and drives us on our knees to pray and cry for revival. Our spiritual eyes see the gulf that exists between what was normative in the Bible and what has become acceptable today.

I have spent hours poring over books on revival and especially *The Hebridean Revival* which began in the tiny village of Barvas on the Isle of Lewis. My bookcase is filled with the works of people greatly used of God such as D.L. Moody, John Wesley, George Whitefield, Charles Spurgeon, Hudson Taylor, Charles Finney, Jonathan Edwards, Evan Roberts, E.M. Bounds, David Brainerd, A.W. Tozer, Murray M'Cheyne and Duncan Campbell. As I scoured their lives, I discovered that they were all burdened with a holy discontent for the status quo and this drove them to their knees in desperate prayer. Holy discontent is that which takes ordinary people and sets them on fire for God. It is the refusal to accept things as they are. It is the determination to make a change in this culture and in the church through the power of Christ and for the glory of God. It is fuelled, not by selfish ambition or financial gain, but a passion to make Christ known to a world that desperately needs it.

Revivals in the pasts trace their genesis to an awakening of God's people to the power of prayer. Today's reading reflects this as the early community of believers embraced the essence of prayer and the place was shaken. The community was shaken and lives transformed.

Chuck Smith gave a searing statement to a church that does not realise its hour:

> *Today, we are living in desperate times. Yet, the Church is not desperate before God in prayer.*[101]

He visits those who recognise their need, who are empty and broken, contrite in heart, who are at the point of desperation, who are panting for Him the way a deer pants for water in the desert. Have we a holy discontent? Are we content to simply *go* to church or do we yearn to *be* the church? Are we content to simply sing another song or do we yearn to engage in worship that the ancient gates would be opened up and the King of Glory come in? Are we content to say our prayers or is there an urgency in our hearts to pray in the Name of Jesus Christ and in His authority and see the darkness pushed back and the demons flee? Are we content to hear another message that will tickle our ears or do we long for ministers to have the Word of God like fire shut up in their bones which they cannot contain? Do you yearn for a sweeping move of God that will turn this nation back to him? May God bring us to our knees.

---

[101] *Effective Prayer Life;* Chuck Smith (2000)

18

Sober Judgement

*"Do not judge, or you too will be judged. For in the same way
as you judge others, you will be judged, and with the measure
you use, it will be measured to you."*

*J*udged anyone lately? Sadly, the answer for most of us (including
me) is – yes. No-one particularly likes to be called judgemental.
When we think of those who are 'judgmental', we think of
hypocritical or self-righteous people. Jesus' words in today's verse were
addressed to the Pharisees. He did not make a blanket statement against
judgment *per se*. He was talking about rash, unwarranted judgments. F.F.
Bruce, a New Testament scholar, explains the linguistic dilemma:

*Judgment is an ambiguous word, in Greek as in English: it may
mean exercising a proper discernment, or it may mean sitting
in judgment on people (or even condemning them).*

It is this second definition, to condemn, that Jesus forbids, and He
makes that clear when the whole sentence in Luke 6 is read:

*"Judge not, and you will not be judged; condemn not, and you
will not be condemned…"*

The Pharisees were quick to see the sins of others but were blind and
unwilling to hold themselves accountable to the same standard they were
imposing on everyone else. The problem was that they had become blind
to their own faults and sin. Jesus added:

*"Why do you look at the speck of sawdust in your brother's
eye and pay no attention to the plank in your own eye? How
can you say to your brother, 'Let me take the speck out of your
eye,' when all the time there is a plank in your own eye? You
hypocrite, first take the plank out of your own eye, and then*

you will see clearly to remove the speck from your brother's eye."

Matthew 7:3-5 (NIVUK)

In other words, deal with your own issues first. Or, as the saying goes, when you point your finger at someone else, there are three fingers pointing back at you.

We must also remember how faulty our perceptions are and how bias distorts our judgment. We often think we understand what's going on, when in reality we do not. Only the Lord can see beyond the outward appearance to underlying motives and causes in a person's heart. I never forget the little lesson shared with me: "Imagine you are walking through a forest and you spot a dog. He looks so cute and friendly. You approach and move to pet the dog. But suddenly he snarls and tries to bite you. The dog no longer seems cute or amiable and you now feel resentment and possibly anger. However, as the wind blows, the leaves on the ground are whipped up and carried away and you see that the dog has one of its legs caught in a barbarous trap. Now you feel compassion and sympathy for the dog. You know the dog became aggressive because he was in pain and was suffering." Never underestimate the pain the person may be enduring. You do not know their backstory.

Judgment is often grounded in arrogance. That's because a judgmental person almost always carries with them a sense of condescension ("I never get into this kind of situation myself...") Paul told us:

I say to everyone among you not to think of himself more highly than he ought to think, but to think with sober judgment, each according to the measure of faith that God has assigned.

Romans 12:3 (ESV)

Remember this: judging someone does not define who they are; it defines who you are.

19

Your Vocal Range

But certainly God has heard me; He has given heed to the voice of my prayer.

Psalm 66:19 (AMPC)

The definition of the word 'voice', according to the dictionary, is 'sound produced in a person's larynx and uttered through the mouth, as speech or song; utter (a speech/sound) with resonance of the vocal cords; the distinctive tone or style of a literary work or author'.

Research shows that most of us have shuddered on hearing the sound of our own voice played back to us. In fact, not liking the sound of your own voice is so common that there's a term for it: voice confrontation. If you have been part of a choir, you will be familiar with the term 'vocal range', usually categorised within six common voice types: Bass, Baritone, Tenor, Alto, Mezzo-Soprano and Soprano. You may even have had a vocal coach.

God loves your voice and its distinctiveness. He encourages us to come to Him with the voice of our prayers, as we saw in today's verse. Prayerfulness is not an event; it is a way of being in relationship with God and expressing ourselves, knowing that God hears us.

The Bible mentions the voice of supplication in Psalm 86:

> *Give ear, O LORD, to my prayer;*
> *And attend to the voice of my supplications.*

Psalm 86:6 (NKJV)

Supplication is humbly and earnestly asking God for something. In Psalm 5 there is mention of "the voice of my cry":

> *Hearken unto the voice of my cry, my King, and my God: for unto thee will I pray.*

Psalm 5:2 (KJV)

The voices of God's children cry out from all over the world, and yet He knows the person behind each voice and responds to every cry. The psalmist mentioned "the voice of my weeping" in Psalm 6:

> *...the LORD hath heard the voice of my weeping.*
>
> Psalm 6:8 (KJV)

In prayer, God hears more than your words – He listens to your heart. He views your tears as liquid prayers.

There is also reference in the Bible to the voice of thanksgiving. Take Psalm 26:7 as an example:

> *That I may proclaim with the voice of thanksgiving*
> *And declare all Your wonders.*
>
> Psalm 26:7 (AMPC)

A heartfelt thank you is always a great conversation starter. Sometimes when our heart is heavy, we rush right into prayer, making our requests known, but we are instructed to make them known with thanksgiving.[102] When we pause to think of all God has done for us, we will have cause to thank Him for His abundant mercies. We can approach Him with "the voice of triumph" as in Psalm 47:

> *...shout unto God with the voice of triumph.*
>
> Psalm 47:1 (KJV)

This is a voice which rejoices in Christ's victory. "The voice of joy and praise" is recognised in Psalm 42:

> *I went with them to the house of God,*
> *With the voice of joy and praise...*
>
> Psalm 42:4 (KJV)

As we take the time to praise God for all He has done in the past – the answered prayers, the impossible situations overcome, the healings and grace – our faith to believe for even greater answers to prayer grows stronger and more confident. Not only was the voice of joy expressed in the house of God; it was heard in the homes of the righteous.

---

[102] See Philippians 4:6-7

The voice of rejoicing and salvation
Is in the tents of the righteous...

Psalm 118:15 (NKJV)

The whole gamut of emotions, the full vocal range, is expressed in the Bible from crying to rejoicing. Let your voice be heard today knowing that He hears and heeds the content of your words and the intent of your heart.

20

Joyful, Patient, Faithful

Be joyful in hope, patient in affliction, faithful in prayer.

Romans 12:12 (NIVUK)

*D*oes this verse describe you, especially when you're going through a difficult trial? I have already asked myself this question and I know there is work to be done, especially in the middle section ("patient in affliction"). How can we put this verse into practice? On 22nd June 1879, in the Metropolitan Tabernacle, C.H. Spurgeon preached a sermon based on Romans 12:12 under the heading 'Constant, Instant, Expectant'. He told us how to apply it to our lives in a way similar to taking medicine. He said the first two phrases – "joyful in hope" and "patient in affliction" – must be taken with prayer. "Joy and patience are curative essences," he said, "but they must be dropped into a glass full of supplication, and then they will be wonderfully efficient."

Let's begin by committing the verse to memory, making it portable and applicable 24/7.

Joyful in hope. Paul was continually rejoicing before God. Why was Paul able to rejoice in hope despite being in situations that seemed hopeless? The Bible tells us that we were "without hope and without God in the world"[103]. But thankfully it describes Jesus Christ as our "only hope"[104]. Without Jesus Christ there is no hope. But in Him we have "a living hope through the resurrection of Jesus Christ"[105] and we have "the blessed hope"[106] of His return. We can surely rejoice in hope because we are saved, forgiven and heaven-bound!

Patient in affliction. Patience is the ability to wait calmly as the Lord works everything in conformity with the purpose of His will. The word

---

[103] Ephesians 2:12 (NIV)
[104] Colossians 1:27 (TLB)
[105] 1 Peter 1:3 (NIVUK)
[106] Titus 2:13 (ESV)

in Greek is *hupomone*. It literally means 'to abide or remain under' but not simply with resignation, rather with a vibrant hope. Paul told us:

> *For our light and momentary troubles are achieving for us an eternal glory that far outweighs them all.*
>
> 2 Corinthians 4:17 (NIVUK)

His hope sustained Paul in his many tribulations.

Faithful in prayer. As those who are faithful in prayer, we will pray not only on schedule but spontaneously throughout the day – "without ceasing"[107] as Paul said to the Thessalonians – a constant communication with Jesus, walking with Him as a continual personal presence in our life. We know prayer is powerful. We know that if we are not faithful in prayer, we cannot be joyful in hope. If we are not faithful in prayer, we cannot be patient in affliction. Consequently, the key to successfully withstanding the seasons of adversity is faithfulness in prayer.

May we apply the medicine of God's Word and may it bring healing to our mental and emotional health and our spiritual well-being.

---

[107] 1 Thessalonians 5:17

21

On Fire for God

Be kindly affectionate to one another with brotherly love, in honor giving preference to one another; not lagging in diligence, fervent in spirit, serving the Lord...

Romans 12:10-11 (NKJV)

One of the primary responsibilities of the priests under the Old Covenant was to keep the fire burning on God's altar perpetually. God expressly commanded them, saying:

A fire shall always be burning on the altar; it shall never go out.

Leviticus 6:13 (NKJV)

In the book of Romans Paul encourages God's people to be fervent and make sure that their fire does not go out. He tells them to be "fervent in spirit; serving the Lord". What does it mean to be fervent in spirit? It means to be on fire for God.

Be on fire with the Spirit. Serve the Lord.

Romans 12:11 (ISV)

Be aglow and burning with the Spirit, serving the Lord.

Romans 12:11 (AMPC)

...keep yourselves fueled and aflame.

Romans 12:11 (MSG)

Fervent. On fire. Aglow and burning. Fuelled and aflame. Our English word 'fervent' comes from the Latin *fervere* which means 'to boil'. This is exactly what the word means in the original Greek (*zeontes*): 'boiling' (in spirit); exhibiting passion. It has everything to do with intensity and devotion for Christ. When you're on fire, your greatest love, your deepest passion and your highest affection is Jesus and His manifest presence.

Paul said:

Do not put out the Spirit's fire.

1 Thessalonians 5:19 (ISV)

Many of us are familiar with the way the King James Version words this phrase:

Quench not the Spirit.

1 Thessalonians 5:19 (KJV)

The word for "quench" literally means 'extinguish or snuff out'. We are not to put out the fire but keep ourselves fuelled and aflame.

Have you ever been camping and had a campfire at night? Often in the morning there will still be coal embers that are in the fire pit. If you want to keep the fire alive, the first thing you do is gather all the coals together. This is why we should never live the Christian life in seclusion. God called us to be in community. Associate with people of passion – people who encourage and inspire you.[108] In Revelation 3 Jesus addressed the Laodicean Church drawing attention to their being lukewarm. It made Him feel nauseated. But keep reading and you find that there was still hope because in verse 19 He says to them:

"Those whom I love I rebuke and discipline. So be earnest and repent."

Revelation 3:19 (NIVUK)

Then in verse 20 He goes further:

"Here I am! I stand at the door and knock. If anyone hears my voice and opens the door, I will come in and eat with that person, and they with me."

Revelation 3:20 (NIVUK)

Jesus extends the same invitation to each one of us so that we can be red hot for God, radiating His presence and power, passionately pursuing what's on His heart. Are you fervent? On fire for God? Aglow and burning? Fuelled and aflame?

---

[108] See Hebrews 10:24-25

22

Behold, the Bush was Burning

The angel of the Lord appeared to him in a blazing fire from the midst of a bush; and he looked, and behold, the bush was burning with fire, yet the bush was not consumed. So Moses said, "I must turn aside now and see this marvellous sight, why the bush is not burned up." When the Lord saw that he turned aside to look, God called to him from the midst of the bush and said, "Moses, Moses!" And he said, "Here I am." Then He said, "Do not come near here; remove your sandals from your feet, for the place on which you are standing is holy ground."

Exodus 3:2-5 (NASB)

The burning bush is a recognised symbol in Irish Presbyterianism. It is embroidered upon countless church pulpits and carved into church tables, chairs and hymn boards all over the country. It is usually accompanied by the inscription "*ardens sed virens*" meaning 'burning but flourishing'. The first 'burning bush' led to a life-changing encounter with God. For Moses, the day began just like any other. He was carrying out a routine task – tending his flock in the wilderness when he noticed a burning bush. This was an ordinary thorn bush, similar to others found in that arid region. It was one among many. However, this bush was ablaze yet strangely did not burn up. It was on fire with God's awesome Presence. When Moses saw the burning bush, he slowed down to pay attention. It actually says he turned aside. Then the next verse tell us that "when the Lord saw that he turned aside to look", He spoke to him. Stephen, in Acts 7, relates this account to us saying:

When Moses saw it, he marveled at the sight; and as he approached to look more closely, there came the voice of the LORD.

Acts 7:31 (NASB)

God wants our attention. In fact, He wants our undivided attention. What if Moses had not responded? What if he had overlooked the bush? How many times do we fail to recognise our 'burning bushes'? God may be speaking to us directly through His Word and our minds are somewhere else. Instead of marvelling at the sight we continue on, clueless. Like Moses, we may be in a desert place but God wants to communicate with us and speak into our lives.

After getting Moses' attention, God's first command to him was for him to remove his sandals. "...remove your sandals from your feet, for the place on which you are standing is holy ground." This is the first occurrence of the word "holy" in the Bible. Moses was to show special honour because of the immediate presence of God. Do we realise that we are standing on holy ground? This Divine encounter effected the deliverance of a nation. God directed Moses to lead the Israelites out of Egypt. He had seen their suffering and Moses would play a part in their liberation. God still speaks into our ordinary lives, transforms everything by His presence and calls us to do His healing and liberating work in the world. It all begins when we turn aside from ourselves and "behold, the bush [is] burning".

23

In Prison Holding the Key

For freedom Christ has set us free; stand fast therefore, and do not submit again to a yoke of slavery.

Galatians 5:1 (RSV)

The Crumlin Road Gaol dates back to 1845 and closed its doors as a working prison on 31st March 1996. After extensive renovations the gaol has reopened as a visitor attraction in Northern Ireland. It is a 19th century Grade A listed building which over the years has housed murderers, suffragettes and loyalist and republican prisoners. It has been the home to executions, escapes, hunger-strikes and riots. On a sevety-minute guided tour, visitors are taken through the years and experience of what life was like for those imprisoned in what is locally called The Crum.

What does freedom mean to you? What does Paul mean when he talks about being "set ... free" in today's verse? Jesus came with the manifesto:

The Spirit of the Lord God is upon me, because the Lord has anointed and qualified me to preach the Gospel of good tidings to the meek, the poor, and afflicted; He has sent me to bind up and heal the brokenhearted, to proclaim liberty to the [physical and spiritual] captives and the opening of the prison and of the eyes to those who are bound.

Isaiah 61:1 (AMPC)

Christ came to set us all free, not only from eternal death, but also from spiritual and emotional imprisonment too. However, too many of us live in self-imposed incarceration by our mindsets. Some live their entire lives in prison, not physically but mentally, a mental prison of their own making, accepting confinement as a norm. Imagine being in prison but having the key in your possession. Surely you would use it to open the lock and walk free? As Christians we have been set free and we need to orient our lives on this truth. Jesus told us:

"If you abide in My word, you are My disciples indeed. And you shall know the truth, and the truth shall make you free."

John 8:31-32 (NKJV)

Again, He said:

"Therefore if the Son makes you free, you shall be free indeed."

John 8:36 (NKJV)

He did not set you free to live the rest of your life in self-inflicted bondage or held hostage by fear, worry and other self-destructive thoughts.

People who have been incarcerated for extended periods may have difficulty adjusting to life outside of prison walls. It may take time after being conditioned to thinking a certain way. Walking out your freedom in Christ will mean taking time to renew your mind, renouncing the lies of the enemy who kept you bound and announcing the truth of who you are in Christ. Have you discovered how amazing your life in Christ is meant to be? William Sleeper in 1887 penned the words:

Out of my bondage, sorrow, and night,
Jesus, I come, Jesus, I come;
Into Thy freedom, gladness, and light,
Jesus, I come to Thee.

Allow Him to set you free and set you in a large place.[109]

---

[109] See Psalm 118:5

24

Doing Good or Do-Gooder?

Beloved, follow not that which is evil, but that which is good. He that doeth good is of God: but he that doeth evil hath not seen God.

3 John :11 (KJV)

*W*e are not saved *by* good works, but to *do* good works. In our society, the term 'do-gooder' has become pejorative; it is a sarcastic putdown of people who are actively doing good deeds in a way that's annoying, interfering and naive. The Free Online Dictionary defines do-gooders as "naive idealists who support philanthropic or humanitarian causes or reforms". But doing good should not be seen in a negative way. Jesus went around doing good:

"You know of Jesus of Nazareth, how God anointed Him with the Holy Spirit and with power, and how He went about doing good and healing all who were oppressed by the devil, for God was with Him."

Acts 10:38 (NASB)

The Greek word for "doing good" means 'to bestow benefits'. The noun form of the word means 'benefactor'. Psalm 37:3 tells us:

Trust in the Lord, and do good; so shalt thou dwell in the land, and verily thou shalt be fed.

Psalm 37:3 (KJV)

Paul stated:

Let us not become weary in doing good, for at the proper time we will reap a harvest if we do not give up. Therefore, as we have opportunity, let us do good to all people, especially to those who belong to the family of believers.

Galatians 6:9-10 (NIVUK)

We are "created in Christ Jesus to do good works, which God prepared in advance for us to do"[110]. Jesus said:

"Let your light so shine before men, that they may see your good works, and glorify your Father which is in heaven."

Matthew 5:16 (KJV)

In Joppa there was a disciple named Tabitha (which, when translated, is Dorcas), who was always doing good and helping the poor.[111] We have the example of the Good Samaritan in Luke 10:25-37 who practically helped a person who had run into bad times. Though he was of different ethnicity, it did not matter to him. Jesus said at the conclusion of the story, "Go and do likewise."[112] Be the good Samaritan. Go about doing good.

Do not withhold good from those to whom it is due,
when it is in your power to act.

Proverbs 3:27 (NIVUK)

To quote John Wesley:

Do all the good you can, by all the means you can, in all the ways you can, in all the places you can, at all the times you can, to all the people you can, as long as ever you can.

---

[110] Ephesians 2:10 (NIVUK)
[111] See Acts 9:36
[112] Luke 10:37 (NIVUK)

25

Familiarity or Friendship

So shall my word be that goeth forth out of my mouth: it shall not return unto me void, but it shall accomplish that which I please, and it shall prosper in the thing whereto I sent it.

Isaiah 55:11 (KJV)

How familiar are you with the Bible? Do you allow your familiarity to breed contempt? We can easily develop familiarity today with the Scriptures and think, "I've heard that before." You've heard and read the same verses countless times. Often your mind can complete the verse as you're reading it or hearing it read aloud. Along with that mental autopilot come years of having heard sermons explaining the meaning of the text. The danger is clear: we can become "dull of hearing"[113]. Paul, however, says to us:

So then faith comes by hearing, and hearing by the word of God.

Romans 10:17 (NKJV)

The word "hearing" is present tense. Jesus said, "He who has ears to hear, let him hear..."[114] because there was something fresh to receive. Each time we look at Scripture, it is fresh and relevant for now. Isaiah 55:11 is an acknowledgement that the words God speaks have impact. They do not "return ... void"[115]. It is a great reminder that God is at work and His words can be transformational in our lives.

We are told:

For the word of God is living and active...

Hebrews 4:12 (AMP)

---

[113] Hebrews 5:11 (ESVUK)
[114] Matthew 11:15 (AMP)
[115] Isaiah 55:11 (KJV)

From the Bible we draw life, strength and power to live the Christian life. Jesus said:

> *...the words that I speak unto you, they are spirit, and they are life.*
>
> *John 6:63 (KJV)*

Unlike great works of poetry or prose, the Bible pulsates with life, for its author is the Creator of the universe, in whom all things consist and in whom we live and move and have our being. Through it, God can unleash power into your life. No matter what we are going through on any particular day, God's Word will be a fresh word of encouragement, challenge and relevance. Don't say, "I heard that before." Allow God to speak afresh into your life.

After His Resurrection, Jesus walked with two disciples on the road to Emmaus. He began to talk to them about the Old Testament, the Law, and the Prophets. It says:

> *Then opened he their understanding, that they might understand the scriptures...*
>
> *Luke 24:45 (KJV)*

As a result, their hearts were burning within.

> *And they said one to another, 'Did not our heart burn within us, while he talked with us by the way, and while he opened to us the scriptures?*
>
> *Luke 24:32 (KJV)*

With the right attitude, God's Word can revive your soul.[116] The unfolding of his words gives light.[117] One verse can be transformative if your goal is to hear the voice of the Holy Spirit.

---

[116] See Psalm 19
[117] See Psalm 119:130

26

A Wide Door

For a wide door for effective work has opened to me, and there are many adversaries.

1 Corinthians 16:9 (ESVUK)

A wide door for effective work has opened. Those words excite me. The apostle Paul used the concept of an open door to illustrate his opportunity to share the gospel. He said:

When I came to Troas to preach Christ's gospel ... a door was opened to me by the Lord.

2 Corinthians 2:12 (KJV)

In the Book of Acts we see Paul and Barnabas gathering the church together and declaring all that God had done and how He had opened a door of faith to the Gentiles.[118] Paul asked to Colossians to pray:

...pray for us, too, that God may open a door for our message ... Pray that I may proclaim it clearly, as I should.

Colossians 4:3-4 (NIV)

The word "door" is equated with 'opportunity'. An open door is an opportunity provided by God, to act with God and for God.

In today's verse Paul says:

For a great door and effectual is opened unto me...

1 Corinthians 16:9 (KJV)

The word "great" is the Greek word *mega*, which always speaks of something that is huge or massive. It is not only great in size, but great in significance. God can do "exceeding abundantly above all that we ask or think, according to the power that worketh in us"[119].

---

[118] See Acts 14:27
[119] Ephesians 3:20 (KJV)

The word "effectual" means 'producing an effect'. The Greek word is *energes* from which we derive our word 'energy'. The door that has opened has a divine release of God's power. It's time to…

> *Enlarge the place of thy tent, and let them stretch forth the curtains of thine habitations: spare not, lengthen thy cords, and strengthen thy stakes; for thou shalt break forth on the right hand and on the left; and thy seed shall inherit the Gentiles, and make the desolate cities to be inhabited.*
>
> *Isaiah 54:2-3 (KJV)*

God is opening doors. We are told in Revelation 3:

> *"I know thy works: behold, I have set before thee an open door, and no man can shut it: for thou hast a little strength, and hast kept my word, and hast not denied my name."*
>
> *Revelation 3:8 (KJV)*

God is the one who opens doors that nobody can shut and closes doors that nobody can open.

A "wide door … has opened to me". There is a natural tendency to think that when God opens doors everything will go smoothly. But God's Word tells us that the opposite is true: when a great and effective door is open, when the potential is there to be really used by God, there will be not a few, but many adversaries to try and stop you. Some may be outside the church; some within.

Nehemiah faced his fair share of opposition when God opened the door for rebuilding the old ruins. His enemies tried different tactics to get him to quit. But he knew he was doing "a great work". In chapter six he sent word to his adversaries:

> *"I am doing a great work, so that I cannot come down: why should the work cease, whilst I leave it, and come down to you?"*
>
> *Nehemiah 6:3 (KJV)*

The good news for us is that when God opens the door, nobody can shut it. Don't get discouraged and weary. If God is for you, who can be against you?

27

Three Months

Thus the ark of God remained with the family of Obed-edom in his house three months; and the Lord blessed the family of Obed-edom with all that he had.

1 Chronicles 13:14 (NASB)

 three-month period figures in a number of biblical passages. For example, Moses' mother was able to conceal her baby for three months.

By faith Moses' parents hid him for three months after he was born, because they saw he was no ordinary child, and they were not afraid of the king's edict.

Hebrews 11:23 (NIVUK)

Jesus' mother Mary visited Elizabeth, Zechariah's wife, and stayed with her for three months.[120] It was during this time that Mary broke out in Spirit-inspired utterance and gave us the Magnificat.

After the ship that was carrying Paul to Rome was wrecked in a storm, he and his captives stayed on the island of Malta for three months.[121] Those three months were spent ministering healing to the locals.

Another example relates to the Ark of God during the time of King David:

The ark of God remained with the family of Obed-Edom in his house three months...

1 Chronicles 13:14 (NIVUK)

And David was unwilling to move the ark of the LORD into the city of David with him; but David took it aside to the house of Obed-edom the Gittite. Thus the ark of the LORD

---

[120] See Luke 1:56
[121] See Acts 28:11

remained in the house of Obed-edom the Gittite three months, and the LORD blessed Obed-edom and all his household. Now it was told King David, saying, "The LORD has blessed the house of Obed-edom and all that belongs to him, on account of the ark of God."

2 Samuel 6:10-12 (NASB)

Few people know about the obscure character called Obed-Edom. He got to host the presence of God and accommodate the Ark in his own home for three months. He opened the door of his home to the Lord – for the Lord to be there 24-7. The Ark of the Covenant was understood to be the presence of God among His people. When the Ark was present, the people knew God was with them. It ended up in his home because the first attempt to move the Ark to Jerusalem ended in the death for one of the Israelites. God had given exact instructions on how the Ark was to be handled, yet when the Ark came back to God's people, they had attempted to move it in an inappropriate way. We read that everything and everyone in Obed-Edom's life was touched by God and blessed. Only three months in the presence of God was enough for people to notice significant and supernatural blessing in his household. The word of God's goodness got out. When the time came to move the Ark to Jerusalem, Obed-Edom had a choice. He could stay where he was and live off his past relationship with God, or he could move with the Ark of God, staying in God's presence and in close relationship with God. His desire for the Lord caused him to do whatever it took to be close to Him. He became a gatekeeper, a musician and a doorkeeper, all roles orbiting around God's presence.

Today we are not only privileged to have God dwell in us; we have the responsibility to carry the presence of God to others. Paul says:

Do you not know that you are God's temple and that God's Spirit dwells in you?

1 Corinthians 3:16 (ESV)

We are temples of the living God. We are containers of His presence. We are carriers of His glory to this generation. His blessings are not to be contained within but shared so that others are blessed around us.

28

Turning the Tide

You've kept track of all my wandering and my weeping. You've stored my many tears in your bottle – not one will be lost. For they are all recorded in your book of remembrance. The very moment I call to You for a Father's help the tide of battle turns and my enemies flee. This one thing I know: God is on my side! I trust in the Lord. And I praise him! I trust in the Word of God. And I praise him!

Psalm 56:8-10 (TPT)

Notice the words, "The very moment I call to You for a Father's help the tide of battle turns." James Hudson Taylor said, "When we work, we work. When we pray, God works." What are you praying and hoping for today? I want to encourage you to stand strong because God is faithful to all His promises, and Scripture tells us that the very moment we pray, the tide of the battle begins to turn.

God has chosen to act in conjunction with our prayers. He freed Israel from Egypt when they cried out.[122] The people of Israel groaned because of their slavery and cried out for help. Their cry for rescue from slavery came up to God and the tide was turned. When we choose to rely on our own understanding and our own limited strength, the waves of life threaten to overwhelm us. Do you need the 'tide to be turned' in your life today? Put your confidence and hope in Him because He who promised is faithful. Know that the tide of the battle is turning. Stand in agreement with His Word.

From one end of the Bible to the other there is the record of those whose prayers have been answered – people who turned the tide of history by prayer. You may be going through a very challenging time, your life seemingly flooded by problems and adversity. Turn to God. He will turn the tide. He will cause you to triumph.

---

[122] See Exodus 2:23

Hear the shouts, hear the triumph songs in the camp of the saved! "The hand of God has turned the tide! The hand of God is raised in victory! The hand of God has turned the tide!"

Psalm 118:15-16 (MSG)

As David turned to God, God turned the tide and he testified:

You have turned my mourning into dancing for me; You have taken off my sackcloth and clothed me with joy, that my soul may sing praise to You and not be silent. O Lord my God, I will give thanks to You forever.

Psalm 30:11-12 (AMP)

Put your trust and confident reliance in God. Stand on His Word. Call out to Him. See the tide of battle turn in your favour.

29

Qarah Moments

So Ruth went out to gather grain behind the harvesters. And as it happened, she found herself working in a field that belonged to Boaz, the relative of her father-in-law, Elimelech.

Ruth 2:3 (NLT)

*I*f you read the book of Ruth, you'll be able to see the fingerprints of God all over her life. The word "happened" in today's verse is the verb *qarah* in Hebrew and we will see that it repeatedly appears in the Bible. Some people mistakenly refer to inexplicable, uncanny, timely happenings as coincidences. But Christians need to recognise them as God-incidences. It is really the gracious hand of the God of providence who is sovereign and good. When Ruth goes out to "gather" in the fields (pick up after the harvesters, as Mosaic law allows the poor to do), she happens to select the field of Boaz. Ruth does not know it yet, but God is weaving the tangled threads of her life together for good. Long story short, Ruth and Boaz end up getting married.

Imagine a huge harvest field without fences or stone walls, yet resembling a patchwork quilt as separate parcels of land within it are assigned to various landowners. The identity of each section of field was linked to the one who owned it. The Amplified Bible says:

And [Ruth] went and gleaned in a field after the reapers; and she happened to stop at the part of the field belonging to Boaz, who was of the family of Elimelech.

Ruth 2:3 (AMPC)

She happened not simply to be in the right field but the right part of the field too.

Can you simply happen to be in the right place at the right time? Was it coincidence that a ram happened to be caught in a bush when Abraham was about to sacrifice Isaac? No, God provided it at exactly the right time. In Genesis 24, we read about how Abraham sent his servant to look for a bride for Isaac, his son. The servant arrived at a well outside the city of Nahor in the evening and decided to stop there. There were so many young women gathered to draw water there that he did not know who would be the right woman for Isaac. So he prayed this prayer:

"O Lord, God of my master Abraham, I pray You, cause me to meet with good success today..."

Genesis 24 (AMPC)

The word "success" here is again the Hebrew word *qarah*. The servant essentially prayed, "Give me *qarah* this day." With the Lord's *qarah,* or right positioning for right happenings, the servant found a beautiful, virtuous woman named Rebekah, who became Isaac's bride. Being in the right place at the right time is orchestrated by the Almighty.

David writes:

The steps of a good man are ordered by the LORD: and he delighteth in his way.

Psalm 37:23 (KJV)

He brought me up also out of an horrible pit, out of the miry clay, and set my feet upon a rock, and established my goings.

Psalm 40:2 (KJV)

God ordered David's steps. May He similarly position us as we pray for *qarah*. I encourage you to pray the prayer of that servant every day. "I pray You cause me to meet with good success today." God will position your path to cross with the right people who will be a blessing to you and to whom you can be a blessing.

30

Arise

Arise, shine, for your light has come,
and the glory of the LORD rises upon you.

Isaiah 60:1 (NIVUK)

William Merrill (1867-1954) penned the words of the old hymn, "Rise up, O men of God! Have done with lesser things. Give heart and mind and soul and strength to serve the King of kings." Men and women of God, it is time to arise. The Amplified translation of today's verse is beautiful:

Arise [from the depression and prostration in which circumstances have kept you – rise to a new life]! Shine (be radiant with the glory of the Lord), for your light has come, and the glory of the Lord has risen upon you!

Isaiah 60:1 (AMPC)

In this crucial time, it's your turn to arise and shine with God's glory. Isaiah 60:1 is challenging us to cast off the doom and gloom. We need to arise as men and women of faith who *know their God*. We need to rise up as men and women of God who *know the times* and realise we are here "for such a time as this"[123]. We need to rise out of religious restrictions; out of trapped traditional mindsets and meaningless ceremony and empty decorum, and raise our voice to preach Christ without apology. Let's rise up with singleness of purpose and one voice, declaring, "Thy kingdom come."[124] Let's renounce all selfish agendas and "seek first the Kingdom of God"[125] and declare, "Thy will be done on earth as it is in heaven."[126] We need to rise up as the "uncompromisingly

---

[123] Esther 4:14 (NIVUK)
[124] Luke 11:2 (KJV)
[125] Matthew 6:33 (ESVUK)
[126] Matthew 6:10 (KJV)

righteous"[127], "oaks of righteousness for the display of God's splendour"[128]. Rise up, realising that we are vessels of honour with *dunamis* in our very DNA, God for us, God with us, God in us! Rise up as people who choose to be relevant, authentic, compassionate and carry the fragrance of Christ to communities. Rise up as those who refuse to be monotone, monochrome, mediocre. We are here to mobilise and let our light shine. We are here to billboard God's greatness and exalt the One who surpasses every superlative. We are here to broadcast in HD[129] God's 4D undiluted love, that all may know its breadth and length and height and depth. How can we sit on the sidelines when resurrection power pumps through our very veins?

The word "arise" has the following meanings: 'to get out of bed, to leave the place or state of rest, or to leave a sitting or lying posture'; 'to emerge from below the horizon, as the sun arises'; 'to begin to act, to exert power, to move from a state of inaction'.

"Arise" is in the imperative mood; in other words, it is a divine demand. To arise is to respond to a command. Circumstances may have kept you prostrate – but no longer. The light has come, and the glory of the Lord has risen upon you. Get out of a reclining state and arise. To arise is indicative of a change. But it is not good enough if we only arise. We must shine, intensify the light and bring hope to an otherwise hopeless world. God did not save us to make us comfortable but rather to use us to do His work of reaching the lost and hurting people of the world. It's His light shining through us that draws those who are lost in darkness.

Are you ready to rise and reflect the light and glory of Jesus? Peter tells us:

> *... you are a chosen people, a royal priesthood, a holy nation, God's special possession, that you may declare the praises of him who called you out of darkness into his wonderful light.*
>
> *1 Peter 2:9 (NIV)*

Paul writes:

---

[127] Proverbs 28:10 (AMPC)
[128] Isaiah 61:3 (NIV)
[129] High Definition

...shine ... like stars in the sky as you hold firmly to the word of life.

Philippians 2:15-16 (NIV)

Times of Refreshing

WINTER DEVOTIONAL

Ruth Gregg

Foreword by Tommy Stewart